Introduction to project management in health research

Introduction to project management in health research

A GUIDE FOR NEW RESEARCHERS

Tim Usherwood

Open University Press
Buckingham • Philadelphia

Open University Press
Celtic Court
22 Ballmoor
Buckingham
MK18 1XW

email: enquiries@openup.co.uk
world wide web: www.openup.co.uk

and
325 Chestnut Street
Philadelphia, PA 19106, USA

First Published 1996
Reprinted 2000

A catalogue record of this book is available from the British Library

ISBN   0 335 19707 8 (pb)   0 335 19708 6 (hb)

Library of Congress Cataloging-in-Publication Data
Usherwood, Tim, 1953–
    Introduction to project management in health research : a guide for new researchers / Tim Usherwood.
        p. cm.
    Includes bibliographical references and index.
    ISBN 0–335–19707–8 (pbk.). — ISBN 0–335–19708–6 (hb.)
    1. Medical care—Research—Management. 2. Industrial project management. I. Title.
    [DNLM: 1. Research—organization & administration. W 20.5 U851 1996]
RA425.U83 1996
362.1'072—dc20
DNLM/DLC
for Library of Congress   96–17727
                                                                    CIP

Typeset by Graphicraft Ltd, Hong Kong

Printed and bound by CPI Group (UK) Ltd, Croydon, CR0 4YY

For Kate, Bo and Sam

Contents

Preface

Research can be many things. It can be fun, boring, satisfying, frustrating, entertaining, tedious, hard work or enlightening. Most researchers probably experience their work in every one of these ways at some time or another. However, good research is never easy. It requires careful planning, rigorous thought and painstaking attention to detail. Even after a precise research question has been defined and clear study objectives formulated, knowledge of appropriate research methodologies is not sufficient for a successful outcome. This knowledge must be put into practice. Those studies that answer their research questions are the ones where the investigators not only have a sound understanding of the methods that they intend to use, but apply them in an effective, efficient and coordinated manner. In other words, they manage the project in order to achieve their objectives, on time and within the constraints imposed by the resources that are available to them.

Much has been written about the methodologies of research; how to undertake a questionnaire survey, how to analyse experimental data, how to collect and explore qualitative data, and so forth. In contrast, very little has been written about the practical problems of managing a research project; how to refine a research question and develop research objectives, and then how to manage activity, time, resources and human relationships in order to achieve those objectives. I hope this book will help to fill the gap.

In writing this book I have been reminded of how much I have learned from my collaborators over the years, especially Linda Gask, David Hannay, Helen Joesbury, Sarah Long, John Stephens and members of the Medical Care Research Unit, Sheffield. They have all taught me more than they realize. Peggy Newton and the publisher's anonymous referees read the text, which has benefited from their many critical and stimulating suggestions. Robert Hebblethwaite and Fiona Macgillivray also gave me useful advice. Jacinta Evans of Open University Press has been a tolerant and encouraging counsellor and guide. The opinions and oversights are, of course, my own.

1

Introduction

Recent years have seen a tremendous increase in research activity concerned with health and health care. Some of this activity is labelled as epidemiology, some as health services research, some as nursing research, some as evaluation research and some by other names. A useful generic term is health research. This book is about the management of projects in the field of health research. Such projects may use methodologies derived from a wide range of disciplines, the social sciences, statistics and operational research for example.

Health research projects that run into difficulties rarely do so because of problems with the research methodologies that have been adopted, but through poor project management. Typical difficulties include running over budget, differences of opinion with key stakeholders, and missed completion deadlines. Many of these problems can be avoided by the application of routine project management methods that are widely used in commerce and industry (see for example Haynes 1989; Geddes *et al.* 1990; Burke 1992) but are less commonly applied to health research. The aim of this book is to offer practical advice on how you can apply project management techniques, including those of budgetary control, time and activity management, management of stakeholder relationships and product marketing, to research. The style of the book is fairly didactic as the intention is to describe a systematic and structured approach that works in practice, and that will help to bring your research to a successful conclusion. Included in the text are a few references to publications which offer helpful advice and guidance on particular methodological and other topics. A small number of other texts that you may find helpful when designing and managing your research are listed at the end of this book.

Most health research is outcome-driven. That is, the investigator seeks to answer a particular research question or questions. He or she may also intend to generate one or more products at the end of the project, such as a bound report or a journal article. This book deals with the management of outcome-driven research. Other research is more concerned with process, and with involvement of participants in every stage of the research. Action research (Hult and Lennung 1980) and 'new paradigm' research (Reason 1988) are examples of the latter. Although outcome-driven research is frequently seen as essentially quantitative in nature, while participatory research is seen as proto-typically qualitative, this is a false dichotomy (Bryman 1988). Many research questions are best addressed using qualitative techniques, leading to specified products (Patton 1990). The resulting studies will therefore be outcome-driven and will be amenable to management as described in this book.

Projects in the field of health research vary enormously in size and complexity. At one end of the scale are small pieces of work involving a single researcher, perhaps without specific funding for the study. Many projects undertaken for masters degrees fall into this category. At the other end are programmes of research undertaken by multidisciplinary teams, lasting several years, with a large budget and often with tight contractual obligations to their funding body. Although the problems of management are more complex in larger studies, the issues and principles remain the same irrespective of size. It is expected that this book will prove particularly useful to nurses, doctors and other professionals at an early stage in their careers as health researchers. Much of it will also be useful to undergraduate and graduate students who are required to undertake research projects as part of their studies. However, the techniques described here can be applied whether you are embarking on your first piece of research or are responsible for a major research contract.

Domains of research project management

Successful management of an outcome-driven research project requires the investigator to pay attention to four distinct domains, or sets of issues:

- study objectives and outputs, and associated quality criteria;
- people and relationships;
- time;
- non-human resources.

Your study objectives are explicit statements of what must be achieved if you are to answer your research question. The outputs are those reports and other products which the project generates. Quality criteria are statements of the standards to which the outputs will be produced; they define the minimum acceptable criteria which the research products must meet.

The people involved in the project are likely to fall into a number of groups, as illustrated in Box 1.1. There will be yourself and any other members of the project team: your co-investigators, project staff and other colleagues. There will be the participants upon whose cooperation most health research depends: patients, survey respondents or others. In addition, there may be other groups of external stakeholders: people who are not members of the project team but whose actions can affect the progress of the project, or who themselves may be affected by the outcome of

Box 1.1 Possible stakeholders in your research

Completion of your project is likely to depend on successful relationships with these people

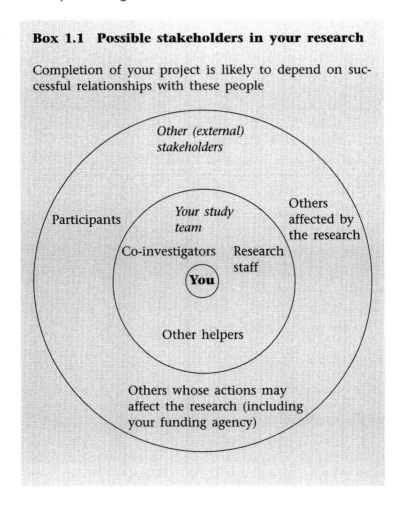

the project. Significant amongst the external stakeholders with power to affect progress are your sources of funds and other resources. Successful completion of the study will require thoughtful management of your relationships with all these people, and of their relationships with each other (Whitaker 1994).

In addition to managing people and relationships, you will need to manage both time and non-human resources (Bennett 1994). Time is significant because most research projects are of a specified duration with a fixed deadline for completion, and because the various activities required to complete the study must be undertaken in some fixed relationship to each other (you cannot start data analysis, for example, until at least some data has been collected). The most significant non-human resource that you will have to manage is money, as this can be used to purchase most of your other requirements.

Although the amount of attention that you will need to pay to each of these four domains will vary as you move through the various stages of your project, none of them will be completely irrelevant at any point.

Phases of a research project

It is convenient to consider a research project as having four phases:

- study definition;
- project planning;
- project implementation;
- project completion.

Study definition starts with the development of a clear, explicit research question and continues with the formulation of well-formed research objectives and the choice of an outline study design. These processes, and some issues specifically concerned with evaluation research, are discussed in Chapter 2. Project planning deals with activity planning, assessment of human and non-human resource requirements, and the preparation of a research protocol. These topics are addressed in Chapter 3. Before you move on to the implementation phase you will also need to consider the issues of research ethics, external stakeholders, funding, and possibly recruitment of project staff. These are discussed in Chapter 4. The implementation of the project is dealt with in Chapter 5 which covers the management of activity,

Box 1.2

Dr Smith has recently been appointed to a university department. She is interested in the benefits of health education for people with asthma. Her progress in addressing this issue will be followed throughout the rest of this book.

time, money and relationships. Chapter 6 addresses the processes of drawing and disseminating conclusions from your study, and marketing the products. It also deals with summative evaluation of the project; what lessons can you take from your project that you will be able to apply to future research?

In order to illustrate the principles and ideas that are described in each chapter, a fictitious research project will be developed throughout the book (see Box 1.2). Although the example is fictional, it contains a mosaic of real experiences. You may disagree with some of the decisions and actions of the people in the example. There is rarely a single right way to undertake any piece of research, and the decisions that are made typically reflect the values, beliefs and previous experiences of those undertaking the project. You are likely to gain useful insights into your own perspectives on the research process through reflection on the possible reasons for differences of opinion between yourself and the fictitious Dr Smith.

2

Defining your research objectives

All research seeks to discover something new about the world, and hence all research projects start with a question. This question may not be explicit and initially may not be clearly expressed, even in the mind of the researcher. However, it is important that you make your research question both clear and explicit, and this chapter will describe how to do this. It will also discuss how to undertake a literature review and to manage the information that this generates, how to refine your research question in the light of the review, how to specify study objectives and how to choose an outline study design. This series of steps is outlined in Box 2.1. The special case of evaluation research, about which there is often confusion, is discussed in the last section of this chapter.

Although research is concerned with answering questions, some books on research methods recommend the formulation of one or more research hypotheses. A study is then designed to test these hypotheses. This approach to defining the aims of a research study has been widely used, and in the case of an experimental design has the advantage of making explicit the null and alternative hypotheses that are to be distinguished in the analysis. However, formulation

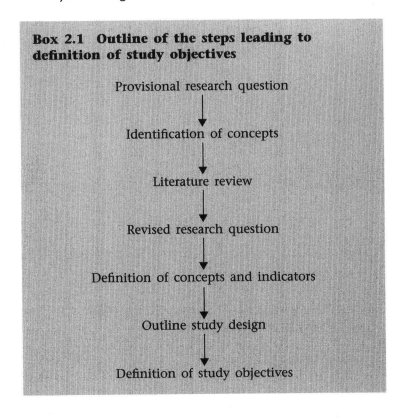

Box 2.1 Outline of the steps leading to definition of study objectives

Provisional research question

↓

Identification of concepts

↓

Literature review

↓

Revised research question

↓

Definition of concepts and indicators

↓

Outline study design

↓

Definition of study objectives

of hypotheses is a somewhat artificial exercise in the case of exploratory or descriptive research, and is not appropriate for certain styles of qualitative research. Even when an experimental design is contemplated, more can be deduced from the findings if they are analysed with a question in mind rather than with the simple aim of distinguishing between hypotheses; modern techniques of data analysis, involving the construction of confidence intervals for example, reflect this approach.

Not only is it essential to generate a clear, explicit research question, it is also important that you care about finding an answer to it. Many studies falter as the researcher begins to lose his or her initial enthusiasm and spends increasing amounts of time doing other things. Research requires self-discipline and a degree of single-mindedness. You may well have a number of reasons for wishing to undertake a particular project, and all of these will provide motivation to continue. However, an important reason is likely to be your personal interest in answering the question that you have posed.

Defining your research question and reviewing the literature

The most creative way of generating an interesting and explicit research question is probably through discussion and debate. You may have a supervisor with whom to explore the area of research in which you are interested. If you work in a university department or similar organization then you may be able to arrange a workshop in which to generate research ideas and possible questions. A number of structured approaches have been described for the development and elaboration of new ideas (Moore 1987). Alternatively, your question may have been posed by others, or may come to you clearly and fully formed as a result of previous research or other experience. However you come by the question, write it down. Even though it may be provisional and you may wish to modify it in the light of further thought and discourse, it will provide a focus for what you do next.

Having written down a provisional research question, you will need to identify the concepts that are represented within it. The concepts are those elements that you will need to define and measure in some way in order to answer the question. They are usually nouns, noun phrases and verbs; see Box 2.2 for an example.

No research is undertaken in isolation from the work of others, so the next step is to undertake a review of the published literature, seeking previous work which has addressed the concepts in your provisional research question. The aims of the literature review are threefold:

Box 2.2

Dr Smith was introduced in the previous chapter. She formulates a provisional research question, as follows:

What are the benefits of health education for people with asthma?

The concepts in this question are;

• benefits
• health education
• people with asthma

• to find out what is already known about each of the concepts that you have identified;
• to find out what is already known in relation to the research question that you have posed;
• to see what research methods others have used in addressing questions similar to your own.

Published literature can be classified into three main groups:

• journal articles;
• books;
• 'grey literature' including reports, governmental publications, theses, etc.

In order to identify relevant publications in all three groups, you will need to undertake several separate literature searches and combine the results. There are several approaches to searching the literature. They include:

• database searching;

- contents scanning and index searching;
- citation searching;
- catalogue searching.

Nowadays a large and growing range of literature databases is available, either online or on CD-ROM. There are various ways of accessing these databases, and if you are not an experienced user then you will need to seek advice from your librarian. Even experienced users may find that new facilities have been added to existing databases, or new databases may become available to them. Most databases allow you to specify a number of keywords, and then to list details of all the publications that these keywords identify. Alternatively, you can specify words or phrases and identify those publications that contain these in their titles. A useful strategy is to identify one or more publications that are clearly relevant to your research question, to note the keywords that have been allocated to these, and then to search for other references which have been allocated these keywords. Another strategy is to identify a seminal early work, perhaps describing an important new research method or finding. Some databases will then allow you to identify subsequent publications that have cited this. It is easy to generate a long list of references using a database, but less easy to include all those that are relevant while excluding those that are not.

One reason for this is that most databases contain only journal articles, which may be drawn from a relatively restricted range of journals. If you suspect that a particular journal contains articles which may be useful to your research, but are unable to access a database in which that journal is listed, then you will need to obtain copies of the contents pages or annual indexes and read through these, seeking titles that appear relevant. Checking the contents pages of recent issues of likely journals can also be useful in identifying recent publications that have not yet been listed in the literature databases to which you have access, and in updating a recent database search. *Current Contents* is useful in this respect. This is a monthly publication that reproduces the contents pages of a range of major journals, and can be scanned in a matter of minutes.

Database searching, even when supplemented by scanning through contents pages and annual indexes, often misses important published articles. This may be because they appeared in journals that you have not covered, or because they were published before the period addressed by your database, or because your search strategy used keywords or phrases that did not identify them. In addition, most databases do not include details of books or reports from the grey literature. A complementary approach to database searching is citation searching. This starts with a recent publication in the area of interest. You read down the list of other publications that are cited in the list of references, identifying those that may be relevant to your own study. You then obtain copies of these, and repeat the process. Obviously it is helpful if you can identify a recent book or review article as a starting point, although a research paper can also be used. The strength of citation searching is that much of the literature that you identify is likely to be relevant. A weakness is that important work may be missed because, for some reason, none of the authors of the papers that you find have cited it. Another limitation is that recent publications are likely to be missed because they have not yet been cited in other works. You should never depend on a citation search alone, but use it to supplement one or more database searches.

Finally, a search of your library's catalogue can be surprisingly fruitful. Most library catalogues, whether based on computer or card index, have some means of identifying books and reports that address particular issues and topics. This may help you identify useful books or items of grey literature which you would otherwise have missed. It does, however, depend entirely on what has been acquired over the years.

In undertaking a literature review you should never depend on any single approach to searching for relevant material. At a minimum it is sensible to combine one or more database searches with a citation search. Some databases include the reference lists of each publication that they list, which allows you to undertake citation searches at the same time as your database search. If you suspect that much of the literature is in the form of books, reports, governmental publications or similar then you will probably need to supplement your other searches with one or more catalogue searches. Library staff are usually very willing to advise further on search techniques. As more information becomes available on the Internet, and as increasing numbers of journals are published electronically, so the help of a librarian is likely to become more valuable in undertaking a search in an efficient and effective manner. You may also be able to identify a specialist library that deals in the area of your research; this may be particularly useful if much of the literature in which you are interested has not been published in readily available journals.

There are a number of ways of handling a growing pile of photocopies, books and other reports. The simplest is to give each a different number, known as an accession number, and to file them in numerical sequence. At the same time, set up a card index or computer database with a separate record for each publication. Each record should contain the accession number, author, title, publishing details and either key words or a short, free-text note of the publication's contents. It then becomes easy to search for a particular reference, or for all the references you have on a particular topic. You can also include in your card index or database details of publications of which you do not possess a copy. Either leave the space for the accession number blank, or use it to identify where a copy is available.

Once you feel that you have successfully addressed the three aims of your literature review as listed above, return to your provisional research question. At this stage you should have a much clearer idea of how the various concepts have been defined, understood and measured by others, and of how others have sought to understand the relationships between them. In the light of your review you may wish to revise your research question somewhat.

Box 2.3

Following her review of the literature, Dr Smith decides to reformulate her research question as follows:

What are the benefits of education about their disease for young adults with asthma?

She lists the following operational definitions and potential indicators for each concept:

Concept: benefits
Operational definition: improvements in health status
Potential indicators:

• mean morning peak expiratory flow rate;
• average daily symptom scores;
• self-perceived health on a quality-of-life questionnaire;
• time lost from work due to symptoms.

Concept: education about asthma
Operational definition: an audio cassette with supporting written material
Potential indicators:

• responses to a questionnaire about time spent listening to cassette and reading material;
• responses to a questionnaire testing knowledge of contents of educational package.

Concept: young adults with asthma
Operational definition: people aged between 20 and 40 years who have recently sought medical treatment for asthma
Potential indicators:

• inclusion in general practitioners' registers of patients with asthma;
• record of consultation for asthma within the preceding six months.

You should also be able to explain why it is important to answer this question.

That done, your next task is to decide exactly how each concept will be defined and measured for the purposes of your project. The definition that you adopt for each concept is often called its operational definition. Those attributes of each concept that you will seek to measure are referred to as indicators. Although you may need to modify both operational definitions and indicators later in the process of planning your research, it is nevertheless important to write them down at this stage (see Box 2.3).

Choosing a study design and defining your objectives

The next step is to choose an outline study design. Most research questions can be addressed in a number of different ways. There is an extensive literature concerning the various approaches to health research, drawing on a wide range of methodologies from the social sciences and elsewhere. These methodologies include both qualitative and quantitative techniques, and a number of useful texts are listed at the end of this book.

It is worth identifying two or three different options for the outline design of your study. You can then list the pros and cons of each and choose a design in the light of these (see Box 2.4). Particularly important issues to consider here are those of gaining access and cooperation. Much health research depends on obtaining access to relevant participants, and then seeking and sustaining their cooperation. It is easy to underestimate the potential difficulties. Obtaining access often involves identifying sources of information about potential participants, and then negotiating permission to use these sources. People who control access to information are known as 'gatekeepers'. Another set of gatekeepers may control access to the participants themselves, and again permission to approach the participants may have

Box 2.4

From her reading and following talks with several members of her department, Dr Smith identifies three possible outline study designs for her research. These are listed below, each with its associated pros and cons:

Design: qualitative evaluation

Outline:
- identify a sample of adult asthmatics;
- provide an educational package to each;
- undertake post-intervention qualitative interviews focusing on sample members' use, knowledge and perceptions of the package, and on self-reported changes in health status.

Advantages:
- small sample;
- relatively quick, provided data analysis is limited to identification of themes and categories (content analysis);
- data would reflect perspectives of participants/users.

Disadvantages:
- changes (if any) in health status not quantified;
- lack of physiological and behavioural data;
- possible acquiescent response set (the tendency of participants to give responses that they think the interviewer wishes to hear).

Design: uncontrolled before-and-after evaluation

Outline:
- recruit a sample of adult asthmatics;
- collect pre-intervention health status data (physiological, functional, symptoms, self-perceived health status);
- administer intervention;

Box 2.4 (cont.)

- collect post-intervention data (as pre-intervention, also use, knowledge and perceptions of the educational package).

Advantages:
- physiological and behavioural data collected in addition to self-perceived health status;
- changes in health status quantified.

Disadvantages:
- larger sample, and longer study than qualitative design;
- no control group.

Design: randomized controlled experiment

Outline:
- recruit sample of adult asthmatics;
- collect pre-intervention health status data (physiological, functional, symptoms, self-perceived health status);
- randomly allocate participants to intervention and control groups;
- administer intervention;
- collect post-intervention data (as pre-intervention, also use, knowledge and perceptions of the educational package from participants in the intervention group).

Advantages:
- physiological and behavioural data collected in addition to self-perceived health status;
- changes in health status quantified;
- control group.

Disadvantages:
- larger sample, and longer study than qualitative design;
- more complicated to organize than uncontrolled before-and-after design.

Box 2.4 (cont.)

After reflecting on the pros and cons of each option, Dr Smith decides to adopt the third, experimental design. Although this will be the most challenging to undertake, and will consume the greatest resources, it will answer her research question most completely and unequivocally.

to be negotiated. For example, in a study of administrative staff working in general practice, you might first have to identify a suitable list of practices. You would then need to obtain permission from the copyright holder of the list to extract contact details of practices. After that you might need to obtain permission from the general practitioners to approach staff working in their practices.

Once you have made contact with potential participants, you have the task of obtaining their cooperation. Participants need adequate information about the aims of the research and what participation will involve. Guidance on the provision of information and obtaining consent is included in the section on research ethics in Chapter 4. However, the important point here is that agreement to participate should be fully informed and freely given. Half-hearted or ill-informed consent may enable the project to start, but participants may subsequently withdraw because they find the commitment too time-consuming, the data collection process too intrusive, or because other issues enter their lives to which they give higher priority (Murphy *et al.* 1992). The process of obtaining access and gaining cooperation can be demanding and time-consuming. These considerations may well have a profound influence on your final choice of study design.

Other considerations that will help to determine your final choice include:

• any constraints that you expect on the financial resources available to support your project;

Box 2.5 Dr Smith's research objectives

- to recruit young adults with asthma to the study;
- to develop an appropriate educational package based on an audio cassette with supporting written material;
- to measure the use made of the package by particip-ants, the knowledge that they gain, and any associated behavioural changes;
- to measure the effects of the educational package on the health status of participants.

- the availability of other non-human resources such as computing equipment;
- the human resources that will be available, along with your own interests, inclinations and areas of research competence, and those of colleagues;
- the time that is available in which to undertake the project;
- any required outputs, such as a thesis or dissertation;
- legal and ethical issues.

These topics are discussed more fully in the next two chapters. A general point worth making is that it is im-portant to choose the study design that will help you to answer your research question most clearly and most completely. If there are unavoidable constraints on time or other resources that prevent you from doing this, then you should consider revising your question in some way. It is better to get a clear-cut answer to a limited question than to ask a more ambitious question and to end up with inconclusive findings.

Having posed your research question in its final form, and chosen an outline design for your study, you can define your research objectives. These are clear, explicit statements of what must be achieved within the context of the out-line study design in order to answer the question that you have posed (see Box 2.5). The objectives should be both sufficient (once all the objectives have been achieved then the question will have been answered) and necessary (if any objective is not achieved then the question will not have been fully answered).

Study objectives fall into two categories: process objectives and outcome objectives. Process objectives are those that reflect aspects of the study design, outcome objectives reflect aspects of the research question. The first two objectives in Box 2.5 are process objectives, the final two are outcome objectives. It is essential to specify a sufficient number of outcome objectives, such that when they are all achieved the research question will have been answered. Some experienced researchers would probably argue that no further objectives need be stated. However, as in the box, it is often helpful to define a small number of key process objectives, achievement of which will be necessary for the question to be answered in the way that is intended. Formulation of process objectives helps to focus thought on what needs to be done prior to the final stages of data analysis and interpretation.

Evaluation research

Evaluation studies differ from other research in that they are concerned primarily with answering questions about a particular service or services (Berk and Rossi 1990). For example, in relation to an innovative project to provide primary health care for homeless people in an inner-city area, evaluation might be concerned with answering questions such as 'How well does this primary health care service for homeless people meet their needs?' The key characteristic of evaluation research is that it seeks to discover the extent to which the service under review meets, or does not meet, the expectations of stakeholders. A number of issues in relation to stakeholders are discussed in Chapter 4, but there are typically three key groups of stakeholders in relation to evaluation research:

- the intended and actual users of the service;
- the people who, through their actions, provide the service;
- the people and agencies who control the resources consumed by the service (and who explicitly or implicitly define the needs which it is intended to address).

The expectations of each of these groups may be tacit, or they may be explicit and expressed in the form of objectives, standards or other text. A number of phrases are commonly used in the definition of expectations by stakeholders:

- the *'quality'* of a service is the degree to which it meets the requirements of its stakeholders (which may be specified as quality criteria);
- the *'effectiveness'* of a service is the extent to which it meets the specified needs of its users;
- the *'efficiency'* of a service measures the resources it consumes in relation to its effectiveness;
- *'value for money'* is an aspiration concerned with achieving maximal efficiency; meeting all the quality criteria at minimal cost.

Even where explicit expectations exist, stakeholders may harbour unstated expectations of the service. If you are planning an evaluation study it is essential to find out as much as you can about stakeholder expectations of the service, as early as possible in the research process. It is also wise to find out as much as possible concerning stakeholder expectations of the evaluation; this issue is discussed further below.

Stakeholder expectations of a service can usefully be considered as referring to four sets of issues:

- structure; this refers to the numbers and qualifications of people providing the service, the buildings and equipment that they use, their records and documentation,

channels of communication, any protocols or guidelines for action, statements of users' rights, and so forth;
- process; this describes the actions taken in providing the service, the ways in which the service is experienced by users, processes of quality assurance and organizational development, processes concerned with equity issues (such as accessibility and equality of opportunity) and the like;
- outcomes; the outcomes of a service are its effects on service users, including their feelings about it;
- inputs; this heading is concerned with consumption by the service of financial and non-financial resources, including people's time.

It is clear that different stakeholders are likely to have different expectations of a service, and that these expectations may not be fully consistent with each other. One way of displaying the expectations of each group of stakeholders in relation to the others is in a matrix, or table, with a row for each stakeholder and columns labelled 'structure', 'process', 'outcomes' and 'inputs'. Incompatibilities and inconsistencies are then readily apparent.

Often the only expectations to have been made explicit before an evaluation study is commissioned are those of the stakeholders who control financial and other resources. One aim of the study may then be to discover the expectations of others. Data on expectations may be collected before data are collected on actual performance, or the two types of data may be collected concurrently. For example, an initial question to service users asking them to identify problems with the service may be followed by further questions seeking details of the problems that they identify, and also by questions asking users to describe what they would wish for instead.

A great danger of evaluation research for the investigator is that of becoming involved in power struggles between different groups of stakeholders. This is particularly likely when the stakeholders have very different expectations of the service. If you do identify significant incompatibilities between the expectations of different stakeholders then your options include the following:

- try to facilitate dialogue between the stakeholders in order to resolve the differences (this may not be practicable, or may not be perceived as your legitimate role);
- undertake the research, make the differing expectations of the stakeholders explicit in your report, and discuss your findings in relation to each (your report may end up being rejected by all);
- decide to withdraw from the evaluation process.

Another danger for the investigator is that of not being clear about the reasons why review of a service is being undertaken. An evaluation project may be commissioned as a contractual requirement, as a basis for planning, to promote service improvements, to document excellence and innovation, or to inform other service providers about the service under review. It is important to be aware of the reasons for the review, and the identities of those who may be required to act in the light of your findings. These may include:

- the service director, and others providing the service;
- the agencies providing resources for the service;
- any organization under whose auspices the service is provided;
- others who provide a similar service, or who are planning one.

More darkly, an evaluation review may be commissioned in order to provide a basis for radical changes or even closure of a service, for reasons which have nothing to do with the need for the service or its effectiveness in meeting that need. Ethically the researcher can only remain true to the defined objectives of the work and to the data that are collected, but it is wise to be aware of the political context of the work.

Despite the potential challenges and conflicts, evaluation work is often interesting and enlightening, and can be very satisfying for the researcher. He or she will probably be expected to make concrete recommendations in the light of the findings, and may have the opportunity of seeing these recommendations translated into action.

3

Planning the research · project

Before starting to plan your research project in detail you should have a clear written statement of your research question and objectives, and a sketch of the outline study design. This chapter will describe the steps that you then need to go through in order to write a full research proposal. It will concentrate on activity planning, assessing your human resource requirements, and the preparation of a budget for the project. The other components of the research proposal will be discussed briefly and an example will be given of a full proposal. The last section of this chapter will address the topic of how to build quality assurance processes into your research. The issues of research ethics, external stakeholders, recruiting and selecting staff, and the problem of obtaining funding will be considered in the next chapter.

Although the process of developing a proposal is presented in this book as linear, with steps following one another in a logical sequence, it is likely that during later steps you will need to reconsider decisions made earlier in the process. Changes made in these earlier steps will then have consequences for other decisions made later in the planning process. For example, you may choose an outline

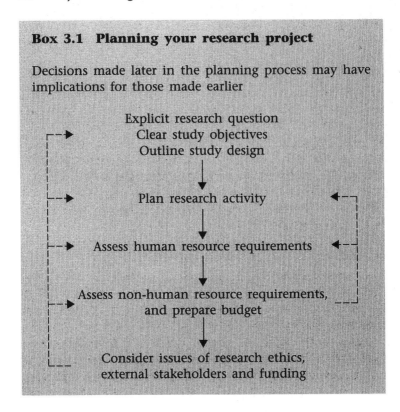

Box 3.1 Planning your research project

Decisions made later in the planning process may have implications for those made earlier

Explicit research question
Clear study objectives
Outline study design

Plan research activity

Assess human resource requirements

Assess non-human resource requirements, and prepare budget

Consider issues of research ethics, external stakeholders and funding

design for your study and calculate a budget as described below, only to realize that the total cost of the project is far beyond what is likely to be available. This may entail substantial changes to the outline design, with consequent revision of your study objectives and subsequent plans. The linear model provides a useful logical framework, but in practice most research planning is cyclical, entailing a number of revisions of the original plan. This is illustrated in Box 3.1.

Planning and scheduling activity

Activity is used here to mean the actions that you or other people working with you on the research will need to perform in order to achieve the research objectives. The first stage of activity planning is to write down a list of all the steps that will be required in order to complete the project. It is important to identify all the activity steps that will be required in order to meet the research objectives. For anything other than a small project it is often useful to involve several people in brainstorming the steps that will be required, in order to ensure that none is missed out.

Once all the activity steps have been identified and listed, you will need to estimate the expected duration of each. Previous experience can be useful here, for example in estimating how long the data analysis is likely to take. A rough calculation may help in estimating the duration of some steps, perhaps based on the findings of a pilot test of the proposed methodology. Once again, you may find it useful to involve others in estimating the expected duration of each step. It is wise to err on the generous side. Box 3.2 gives an example of a list of activity steps and their estimated durations.

The number of participants that you decide to involve in the study is likely to have a profound effect on the duration of several of the activity steps, and thus of the project as a whole. You will therefore need to decide at an early stage the size of any sample that you will recruit. It is important that this decision has a rigorous basis. Failure to specify an appropriate sample size, and to justify this, is a common reason for lack of success in obtaining funding. Those studies that succeed in starting without prior specification and justification of sample size frequently fail to finish, or to answer their research questions.

For quantitative designs, the sample size is calculated on the basis of the desired statistical power of the study (Florey 1993). In the case of a survey, this is defined in terms of the precision with which means or other summary statistics can be estimated from the data (Yates 1981; Gardner and Altman 1989). In experimental and similar designs, power reflects the probability of correctly rejecting the null hypothesis of no difference in outcome between intervention and control groups, when an intervention effect exists (Judd

Box 3.2

Following advice from a statistician on the required number of participants in her study, Dr Smith and two colleagues list the activity steps that they identify as being necessary for her project, and the estimated duration of each.

Activity step	Estimated duration (weeks)
1 produce an educational audiotape	8
2 produce written material	4
3 obtain approval from research ethics committee	8
4 recruit GPs who are willing and able to help	8
5 draw sample of young adults with asthma	2
6 develop and pilot questionnaires and symptom diary	8
7 recruit participants and obtain informed consent	16
8 obtain pre-intervention health status data	4
9 code and enter data on computer	4
10 randomize participants to intervention and control groups, and distribute educational package to participants in intervention group	2
11 wait for changes in health status, if any, to develop	12
12 obtain post-intervention data	4
13 code and enter data on computer	4
14 analyse data, draw conclusions and prepare recommendations	12
15 write up project report	8
16 thank participants and their GPs	2

and Kenny 1981; Armitage and Berry 1987). When planning the size of your intended sample, you should bear in mind that a proportion of those whom you approach will not wish to participate in your research, or will subsequently withdraw. You will need to contact more people than will actually participate. It is important to allocate time and other resources to encouraging participation. In a survey, for example, you should normally allow enough time to follow up non-respondents on at least two occasions after your initial contact. A smaller sample with a high response rate is generally preferable to a larger sample with a low response rate (see Abramson 1984 and Dillman 1978 for further advice on survey methods).

The sampling method, and the resulting sample size, in a study using qualitative methods will reflect the question that is being addressed and the context in which it is being asked. Sometimes it is not possible to do more than identify a sample of convenience, based on those potential participants who can be readily identified. Wherever possible, the sampling process should reflect the purpose of the research more closely; it should be purposive. A wide variety of purposive sampling schemes have been described (Patton 1990). Kuzel (1992) has listed the key characteristics of many of these:

- Sample units are selected serially. Who comes next depends on who came before, and what was learned from them.
- The sample is adjusted continuously or 'focused' by the concurrent development of a theory or understanding of the social processes under investigation.
- Selection continues to the point of redundancy, when no fresh insights are obtained from newly selected participants.
- Sampling includes a search for negative cases in order to test the developing theory and to extend its range of application.

One example of purposive sampling is maximum variation sampling (Patton 1990), in which participants are sought to represent as wide a variety as possible in relation to those dimensions which may be relevant to the research. Another example is theoretical sampling, employed in grounded theory methodology (Strauss and Corbin 1990). In this, data collection, analysis and interpretation proceed concurrently, with new participants constantly being sought whose data might help to develop further the theory that is being constructed. The process ceases once no further insights are obtained from new recruits. This point is known as 'theoretical saturation'. Although theoretical sampling represents a methodologically rigorous approach, it does create problems for the researcher at the stage of planning the project. Because the final sample size depends on what is discovered during the data collection, analysis and interpretation process, there is no sound a priori basis on which to estimate how many participants will be required, or how long the whole process will take. This may be one reason why maximum variation sampling is often employed in its stead. Alternatively, the researcher may just have to hazard a guess at numbers and the time that will be needed.

Having listed all the activity steps in your project, and estimated the time that each will take, you will be in a position to prepare a timetable for the project and to estimate its total duration. A useful tool here is the Gantt chart, illustrated in Box 3.3. A Gantt chart is prepared by listing all the activity steps of the project in a column on the left-hand side of a sheet of paper. Starting with the earliest activity that must be undertaken, a horizontal line is drawn to the right. The line starts at time zero and the length of the line represents the expected duration of that activity. The next activity to be undertaken is then identified and a horizontal line of appropriate length is drawn starting at a point which corresponds to completion of the first activity. The process continues like this for subsequent steps. Where more than one activity can be undertaken at the same time then this is indicated by the presence of parallel lines. For example, in Box 3.3, steps 1, 3 and 4 can all be undertaken concurrently during the first eight weeks of the

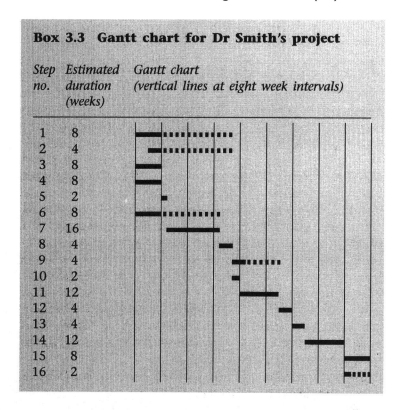

Box 3.3   Gantt chart for Dr Smith's project

Step no.	Estimated duration (weeks)	Gantt chart (vertical lines at eight week intervals)

project. On the other hand, step 5 (draw sample) cannot start until the GPs have been recruited (step 4).

Another feature of the Gantt chart illustrated in Box 3.3 is the use of dotted lines to show where an activity may be undertaken later than indicated by the solid line. The dotted line is continued up to the point where an activity that depends on its completion is to start. An example is step 9 in the box, indicating that data coding and entry following the pre-intervention data collection may be undertaken at any time up to the point at which post-intervention data collection commences (step 12). The dotted lines in a Gantt chart are inserted after all the solid lines have been entered.

A Gantt chart is a useful planning aid. It can be used to calculate the total expected duration of the project. If this will be more than a few weeks then an appropriate amount of extra time should be added to allow for annual leave. The chart also permits ready identification of the activities that will be undertaken at any particular point in time. Where more than one activity is intended at some point then you should check that you will have sufficient resources available. Referring to Box 3.3 for example, Dr Smith will need to ensure that she has the time to undertake steps 1–4 (produce material, obtain ethical approval and recruit GPs) and step 6 (develop and pilot questionnaires and symptom diary) concurrently. Otherwise she will need either to obtain additional help, or to postpone work on step 6. The dotted line indicates that the second option is possible as the questionnaires and diary will not be required until step 8 (obtain pre-intervention data). Similarly, although step 9 (data coding and entry) is time-tabled to start at the same time as step 10 (randomize participants and distribute educational package) it is clear from the chart that the former activity could be delayed to a quieter time, step 11 (wait for changes in health status to develop), without increasing the overall duration of the study. The Gantt chart will also be of use during the implementation phase of the project, when it can help in monitoring actual progress against what has been planned. This will be discussed further in Chapter 5.

Assessing your human resource requirements

As you go through the process of planning and scheduling the activity steps needed to complete your project, so you will begin to develop an understanding of the human resources that you will require. It may be that you have both the time and the skills to undertake the whole study yourself. Alternatively you may see the need to employ one or more assistants to work with you on the project. Such project staff may be employed throughout the duration of the project or may be recruited to help at particular times.

As an example of the former situation you may require someone who can offer administrative and secretarial support. As an example of the latter case, it is not uncommon in projects requiring data collection by interview to employ a group of interviewers for the relevant phase of the project. Subsequently one or more people may be employed to code and enter the data that the interviewers have collected.

It is useful to think about your requirements for project staff in terms of the answers to three questions:

- When do you need help? Think about each of the activity steps in turn. Unless you have both the time and the skills to undertake that step yourself, you will need some form of assistance.
- How many people do you need? Once you have identified the activity steps with which you will need help, you can estimate how much help you will require.
- What skills will they need to possess? The answers to this question will be determined by the nature of the activities with which they will be concerned, by the skills that you personally are able to bring to the project, and by the amount of time that you will have available for supervision; if this will be limited then you may need to recruit staff with more skills and experience than if you can give unlimited time for supervision.

The goal is to ensure that you will have sufficient people to undertake each activity step and that between you all, you will have both the time and the skills to do so.

Having assessed your requirements for project staff, you will need to consider precisely how you are going to ensure that the right staff are available at the right times during the study. The choice is likely to be between recruiting staff on fixed term contracts, paying an agency to provide staff, and obtaining help from existing staff within your organization. You should consider the pros and cons of each. Staff recruited on a fixed term basis will be able to focus all their energies on your research but may be distracted by the problem of finding further employment in the future. Staff who are employed via an agency are likely to prove more expensive and may have little commitment to your particular project. However they can be a flexible resource as you can specify to the agency exactly when you want assistance and what skills the people should have. Friends and colleagues within your organization may bring a great deal of goodwill but are likely to have their own agendas and may have pressures on them that they prioritize higher than the success of your project.

You should write an outline job specification for each member of your team who will be employed either directly or via an agency. If you subsequently have to advertise any of the posts then this outline can be expanded in preparation for the recruitment and selection process, as discussed in Chapter 4. At this stage, however, it is sufficient to specify your requirements for each member of the project staff under the following headings:

- duration of post;
- hours per week;
- duties.

See Box 3.4 for an example.

Preparing a budget

The next task in planning your research project is to prepare a budget. A budget is a statement of the expected costs of the various resources that will be employed (Hopkins 1994). Those costs that will be incurred only as a result of undertaking the project are described as direct (or variable) costs. Those costs that will be incurred whether or not the project goes ahead are referred to as fixed costs.

Start by identifying your direct costs. In general these will fall into three categories: capital costs, staff (human resource) costs, and other direct costs (see Box 3.5). Capital costs are incurred through purchases of equipment that

**Box 3.4 Outline job specification for
Dr Smith's research assistant**

Dr Smith decides that she will need help at a number of
stages of her project. She will not have the time to do
everything herself and she has limited typing skills. After
reflection she writes the following outline job specification:

Duration of post
Eighteen months (i.e. 78 weeks. The estimated duration
of the project is 72 weeks, plus six weeks for annual leave).

Hours per week
50 per cent part time, hours to be negotiated.

Duties
To be responsible to Dr Smith, the project leader, and to
undertake such duties as she directs including:

• liaising with local general practitioners;
• contacting, visiting at home and recruiting study participants;
• preparing and distributing questionnaires and other
  material;
• coding and entering data on computer;
• assisting with data analysis;
• assisting with preparation of final report including word
  processing and simple desk-top publishing.

**Box 3.5 Classification of the costs of a
research project**

• Direct costs — capital costs
                — staff (human resource) costs
                — other direct costs
• Contribution to fixed costs (overheads)

will be needed for the project, such as a computer and associated software. Staff costs include salaries, employer's superannuation contributions, and any other costs to the employer (such as National Insurance contributions in Britain). Your outline job specifications will provide the basis for deciding on appropriate salary scales, and you should seek advice to ensure that any new appointments are made in accordance with your organization's salary structure and policies. Allowance should be made for annual salary increments where appropriate, and many funding agencies also expect an allowance to be made in the budget for wage inflation. Some however require the budget to be calculated on the basis of current costs and agree to fund nationally-agreed wage increases should these occur. Staff costs may also include recruitment costs (including advertising) and contributions to redundancy payments.

An efficient way of identifying and calculating your other direct costs starts with a sheet of paper with rows and columns. Graph paper is useful here. Alternatively you can use computer spreadsheet software. Along the top list the activity steps that you have identified. You may also wish to include a column for the costs of disseminating your findings and marketing the products of your study (these activities are discussed in Chapter 6). Down the side list the various types of cost (budget headings) that these activities will incur. Examples might be postage, telephone, photo-copying, travel and subsistence. Now calculate or otherwise estimate the cost that will be incurred under each activity in relation to each budget heading, and enter your estimate in the appropriate box. Finally, add up the figures in each row to estimate the total other direct costs of your project (see Box 3.6).

You will now be in a position to prepare a statement of the expected direct costs of your project. This will provide the basis of your final budget. The remainder of the budget will be concerned with your fixed costs. These are costs that will be incurred by you or your organization irrespective of whether the study is undertaken. They are sometimes referred to as overheads. Most universities and many

Box 3.6 Dr Smith's spreadsheet used for calculating her other (non-staff, non-capital) direct costs

The columns associated with activity steps that will not generate other direct costs are suppressed in this box.

Budget heading	Activity step											Total
	1	2	4	6	7	8	9	10	12	15	16	
Recording studio	900	0	0	0	0	0	0	0	0	0	0	900
Audiotapes	300	0	0	0	0	0	0	0	0	0	0	300
Peak flow meters	0	0	0	0	960	0	0	0	0	0	0	960
Stationery	0	100	20	20	20	50	10	10	50	50	20	350
Printing and copying	50	400	0	10	10	80	0	10	80	200	10	850
Postage	0	0	20	10	0	200	0	80	200	0	60	570
Telephone	0	0	50	20	40	40	0	0	0	0	0	150
Travel and subsistence	100	0	50	90	200	0	0	0	0	0	0	440
Total	1350	500	140	150	1230	370	10	100	330	250	90	4520

other organizations will seek to include a contribution to fixed costs in the budget of any proposed research project. The basis upon which this contribution is calculated varies widely and you will need to obtain advice about this from your own organization. However, the attitude towards the inclusion of a contribution to fixed costs within a research budget also varies from one funding agency to another. The majority of smaller charities, for example, refuse to make any contribution to fixed costs; a few of the larger charities will make some contribution. Government departments and other public sector organizations in Britain typically have a fixed formula with which to calculate the maximum contribution that they are prepared to make. Commercial organizations are the least predictable as they will seek to commission research at the lowest price that meets their objectives and quality criteria. Obviously the amount of contribution to fixed costs then becomes a matter of negotiation, and when dealing with commercial organizations it may be preferable to quote only the total price for the research. This effectively denies their negotiator the opportunity to haggle over the costs of individual elements of the budget. In Britain, at least, research undertaken in contract with a commercial organization is often subject to Value Added Tax (sales tax) and this should be specified in the quotation.

The final version of Dr Smith's research budget is shown as part of Box 3.7. The contribution to overheads has been calculated at 40 per cent of total staff costs as this is the maximum that the funding agency is prepared to meet.

Other components of the research proposal

Once you have developed a timetable for your project, with the aid of a Gantt chart or otherwise, and have calculated the budget, you will be in a position to prepare a final version of your study proposal. This is always worth doing, and is essential if you intend to make a submission for funding. Box 3.7 shows the typical components of a submission, but funding agencies vary somewhat in their requirements in respect of layout and other details, and up-to-date information should be obtained from wherever you hope to obtain support.

The introduction to a proposal describes the background to the study and makes the case for undertaking it. What gap in current knowledge will the research fill? Why is it important to answer the research question? The question itself and the study objectives are clearly stated. The methods section describes exactly what will be done and includes a Gantt chart or timetable. The size of any samples must always be justified and it is often necessary to justify other aspects of the intended methodology. The intended products and other outputs of the project should be stated.

Legal and ethical issues should be addressed. These typically include issues of confidentiality and the implications of data protection legislation. Much health research requires approval from a research ethics committee, and funding agencies will require evidence that this has been obtained. The role and function of research ethics committees are discussed further in Chapter 4.

If there is any possibility that your project will lead to a marketable product or other commercially important outcome then the proposal must also address the issue of intellectual property rights. At the very least it should make clear who will own the copyright of any textual or graphic material that is produced. However, the laws of copyright and intellectual property are complex, and you should seek local, up-to-date advice.

Even if you do not expect any commercially important outcomes from your project you should consider who will have the right to publish the findings, and who might expect to be included as an author in any research reports. Unless these issues are totally clear both to yourself and anybody else who is involved, you should take steps to clarify them. It may be appropriate to specify in your proposal the intended authorship of any reports. Alternatively, you may need to negotiate and keep a separate memorandum of agreement. Arguments at the end of a study over the right to publish and over authorship are a major cause of discord between researchers, and are readily prevented.

The layout of the budget statement may have to be modified somewhat in order to comply with the requirements of the funding agency, and justification may be required for certain elements of this. Finally, most funding organizations require a brief curriculum vitae from the investigator and anyone else directly involved with the project.

On reading the example given in Box 3.7 you may feel that you would have designed the study somewhat differently. There is probably never such a thing as an ideal design to answer any research question. Instead, there are likely to be a number of designs, each of which could be implemented and if undertaken would answer the question. The choice between these designs will be constrained by the resources that are available, and may also depend on the skills, experience and preferences of the investigator. If you identify aspects of Dr Smith's proposal with which you disagree then something may be learned from reflecting on the strengths and weaknesses of what she has proposed, and of any alternatives that you identify.

Building quality assurance into your study

Quality assurance refers to the process of ensuring that each activity contributing to the completion of your project is undertaken to a standard sufficient that your question is fully answered, that your findings are valid, that your objectives are achieved, and that any quality criteria specified for your research outputs are met. Choice of an appropriate study design, careful application of your chosen research methodology, and painstaking attention to detail are clearly essential in this regard, but it is also worth considering how you might build dedicated quality assurance processes into your study. These need not be elaborate, but

Box 3.7 The final proposal for Dr Smith's project, ready for submission

Introduction

(This is not reproduced here in full. It describes the background to the research, explains in what ways the study will contribute new knowledge, and emphasizes the importance of answering the research question.)

Research question

What are the benefits of education about their disease for young adults with asthma?

Study objectives

- to recruit as participants young adults with asthma;
- to develop an appropriate educational package based on an audio cassette with supporting written material;
- to measure the use made of the package by participants, the knowledge that they gain, and any associated behavioural changes;
- to measure the effects of the educational package on the health status of participants.

Methods

The study uses a randomized controlled trial design, and will be undertaken in five phases:

- production of an educational package based on an audiotape with supporting written material;
- recruitment of participants and pre-intervention data collection;
- allocation of participants to intervention and control groups and distribution of educational package to members of the intervention group;

Box 3.7 (cont.)

- post-intervention data collection;
- data entry and analysis.

Production of educational package

This will comprise an audiotape with supporting written material. The audiotape will address the following topics:

- causes, pathophysiology and symptoms of asthma;
- drug treatment of asthma;
- responding to acute symptoms and respiratory tract infections;
- active and passive smoking;
- common fears.

Each of these topics will be addressed in a fairly didactic manner in a short programme lasting between 10 and 15 minutes. The written material will be divided into sections, each section supporting one programme. Both the tape and written material will be attractively packaged and produced to a high quality.

Recruitment and pre-intervention data collection

A number of local general practitioners (GPs) will be approached and their cooperation sought. Those who have a register of patients with asthma and who agree to cooperate will be included in the study. The GPs' practice staff will review the medical records of patients whose names are included in their asthma registers and who are aged between 20 and 40 years. Those who have a record of consultations for asthma within the preceding six months will be invited to participate. They will be contacted by the GP by letter or telephone and if they express interest will be visited at home by a research assistant. The research assistant will give a full explanation of the study and if the patient agrees to take part, then s/he will be

Box 3.7 (cont.)

asked to sign a consent form. S/he will then be taught how to use a peak flow meter and one of these will be left with him/her for subsequent use.

In order to have an 0.8 probability of detecting a clinically significant intervention effect at the $P < 0.05$ significance level, 60 participants will be required in each group (see Appendix 1 for power calculation). In order to allow for a drop-out rate of up to 25 per cent, participants will continue to be recruited until a total of 160 have agreed to take part in the study.

Once the target of 160 participants has been reached, each will be mailed a questionnaire and a diary for self-completion. The questionnaire will address the following areas:

- current medication;
- recent time lost from work due to asthma symptoms;
- self-perceived health (using a quality-of-life questionnaire).

The diary will be completed on a daily basis for 10 days to record:

- pre-bronchodilator morning peak expiratory flow rate;
- nocturnal symptoms;
- daytime symptoms;
- medication.

Participants will be asked to return the questionnaires and diaries in a stamped addressed envelope. Non-respondents will be followed up by a telephone call and/or home visit.

Allocation to intervention and control groups, and distribution of educational intervention

Participants will be allocated to equal-sized intervention and control groups by a process of simple randomization. On receipt of their completed questionnaires and diaries,

Box 3.7 (cont.)

participants in the intervention group will be sent the educational package with a covering letter. Participants from the control group will be sent a letter of thanks. No further contact will be made with participants for 12 weeks in order to give them time to use the package, make any changes in their behaviour, and for any consequential changes in their health to develop.

Post-intervention data collection

Exactly 12 weeks after the last intervention package has been posted, all participants will be sent a second questionnaire for self-administration plus a diary for self-completion covering the same topics as before. In addition, participants in the intervention group will be sent a questionnaire which addresses the following:

• time spent listening to audiotape and reading accompanying material;
• knowledge of contents of educational package;
• behavioural changes that they have made as a result of the educational intervention.

Once again, non-respondents will be followed up by telephone call and/or home visit.

Data entry and analysis

Data from the questionnaires and diaries will be entered on a computer and analysed using the Statistical Package for the Social Sciences (SPSS). The principle analysis will entail comparisons between intervention and control groups before and after the educational package was distributed. Student's t-test, the Wilcoxon rank sum test and the chi-squared test will be used as appropriate.

Box 3.7 (cont.)

Outputs

The outputs of the project will include the following:

• a full project report;
• an educational package for young adults with asthma;
• a paper suitable for publication in a peer-reviewed journal.

Timetable

The total duration of the project will be 18 months. Details of the proposed timetable are given in the Gantt chart in Appendix 2.

Legal and ethical issues

Approval for this study will be sought from the local research ethics committee. Questionnaires, diaries and other documents will be stored in locked filing cabinets. Patients will be identified by a code number only in data held on computer, and the requirements of the Data Protection Act will be complied with.

Budget – 1 January 1994 to 30 June 1995

Salary for research assistant	12 064
(18 months 50 per cent part time, grade 1B point 3)	
Superannuation and National Insurance	3 137
(employer's contributions)	
Computer, printer and software	2 000
Recording studio	900
Audiotapes	300
Peak flow meters	960
Stationery	350

Box 3.7 (cont.)

Printing and copying	850
Postage	570
Telephone	150
Travel and subsistence	440
Contribution to overheads	6 080
Total	27 801

References

(Not reproduced in this box)

Appendix 1

(Not reproduced in this box)

Appendix 2

(See Box 3.3)

can add substantially to the confidence that you and others will have in the outcomes.

A number of quality assurance processes are commonly used in research:

• instrument validation; the findings of studies in the quantitative tradition are predicated on the validity of the instruments (questionnaires, checklists, rating scales and the like) that are used to collect data. Even if you decide to use a previously validated instrument, you should ensure that it has been shown to give valid data in your own context; if it has not then you should consider undertaking a validation study before the study to answer your specific research question. In the qualitative methodologies the investigator is in many ways the measuring instrument, and there is a strong tradition in anthropology and other disciplines of critical self-reflection in order to explore and make explicit the investigator's beliefs, values, assumptions and feelings;

- triangulation; this refers to any of a number of ways of checking data collected from one source with that collected from another source. Questionnaire data about health service use, for example, might be compared with attendance data, or information from one respondent might be compared with that from another. Such comparison need not necessarily be undertaken in respect of all study participants; it often suffices for quality assurance purposes to check that similar data is obtained from the second source in a representative subsample of the participants;

- double coding; research data, whether numerical, textual or otherwise, often requires coding before further analysis is possible. This process is prone to mistakes and inconsistencies so that many investigators routinely arrange for all data to be coded at least twice, checking for discrepancies between the first and second coding passes. If it is not possible to recode all data, then it may be possible to do this for a sample and to document the proportion of discrepancies that occur;

- double data entry; similar considerations apply to the process of data entry, especially in respect of quantitative data. Once again, re-entry is possible to locate discrepancies and to document their frequency. Many data entry and analysis software packages can support data checking of this kind. They may also provide logical data checking, to ensure for example that text is not entered in a field where numbers are expected, or several digits where only one is required;

- data audit; this is the process of checking the whole process of data collection, recording, coding and entry in respect of a small number of research participants, as a test of the quality of this process across all participants;

- measurement of the intervention; in the case of research to assess the impact of some kind of intervention, it is important not merely to measure those variables that the intervention may influence if it is effective, but also to measure variables that reflect the intervention more directly. For example, the third objective in Dr Smith's study starts 'to measure the use made of the package by participants' (Box 3.7). Following the intervention, participants in the intervention group will be sent a questionnaire which addresses time spent listening to the cassette and reading the written material;

• check analysis; before the widespread use of computers for statistical analysis, various check analyses were routinely used. Even today, it is worth considering whether to ask a colleague to check crucial aspects of such an analysis. Parallel analysis by a colleague of a qualitative dataset can also be valuable, and often generates new and unexpected insights; such parallel analysis is sometimes called 'analytical triangulation'.

You may be able to devise other quality assurance processes for your own study. If so, it is worth considering incorporating them in your project. Good quality assurance has high added value; it costs little in terms of time and other resources, but adds significantly to the quality of the final product.

4

Research ethics, external stakeholders, obtaining funding, and recruiting and selecting staff

During the planning phase of your project you should think about the ethical implications of your research. How will it affect your study participants and other stakeholders? What are the implications for the design and implementation of your project? Is research ethics committee approval required for your study? These issues are addressed in the first section of this chapter.

Also during the planning phase you should think about how you are going to relate to your external stakeholders: those people who are not members of the project team but who nevertheless have influence or an interest in the project. The second section of this chapter addresses the topic of your external stakeholders. The next section briefly reviews the issue of obtaining funding for your study, and the final section discusses the process of recruiting and selecting research staff.

Research ethics and ethics committees

Virtually all research raises ethical issues, but these are most obvious in the context of health research. Ethics is concerned with appropriate and responsible behaviour in our relationships with others and with the world in which we live. Most ethical codes are deontological; that is, they are based on absolute moral principles. A useful framework for considering ethical questions in research is based on the following principles:

- respect for autonomy; people have the right to make informed decisions about matters that affect themselves;
- non-maleficence; the obligation not to do harm;
- beneficence; the obligation to do good if possible;
- justice; resources should be allocated and applied fairly and equitably.

The ethical questions that arise in health research can be grouped under three headings:

- scientific validity of the research;
- autonomy of research participants;
- welfare of research participants.

The first heading covers questions such as 'Is it necessary and important to answer the research question?' and 'Will this study provide a valid answer?' At first sight these may not seem to be questions so much of ethics as of scientific validity and research methodology. However, it is not ethical to inconvenience research participants, or to put them at risk of discomfort or harm, if the study seeks to answer a trivial question or if the design is such that a valid answer is unlikely. To do otherwise is likely to breach the principles of non-maleficence and beneficence. If the research question is important and a poorly designed study goes ahead there is a risk that the conclusions and recommendations will be acted upon without regard to their validity. Again, harm may result. In addition, many research participants take it on trust that the study with which they are assisting is valid and useful. Abuse of this trust countervenes the principle of respect for autonomy. Finally, the investment of research funds and other resources in poor or irrelevant studies reduces the resources available to support other, potentially better research, and runs counter to the principle of justice.

The second set of questions are concerned with participants' rights to make informed decisions about matters that affect them. How will data be collected? From whom will consent be sought, and how? How will confidentiality be ensured? Consent is always needed from participants, and this must be preceded by explanation of the purpose of the research and its implications for the participant. The following topics should be addressed:

- the purpose of study;
- what will be involved for participants;
- what other information will be collected (from medical records, for example);
- potential discomfort or harm to participants;
- for patients, the implications for their care of choosing to participate, and of choosing not to participate;
- a participant's right to withdraw at any time, without giving a reason, and without prejudice in any way;
- what will happen to the data that is collected and how confidentiality will be maintained.

Any verbal discussion of these topics should be supported by written information. The information sheet should read clearly and simply and should avoid technical jargon. Wager *et al.* (1995) have given a checklist of points to bear in mind:

- use short sentences;
- avoid jargon, or explain it when necessary;
- lists are clearer than paragraphs of text;
- a question and answer format can be useful;

- headings help the reader by breaking up the text;
- everything in capitals is less legible than use of upper and lower case;
- serif typefaces are easier to read than sans serif;
- black text on a white background is usually clearest;
- use at least 12-point font size.

If people from a non-English speaking background are to be invited to participate, then the information sheet must be available in appropriate languages. Box 4.1 gives an example of an information sheet for participants in Dr Smith's study.

Occasionally it may be reasonable to seek only verbal consent, or to assume that consent is implied by the act of participation in the study. An example is where data collection is by postal questionnaire; return of a completed questionnaire is often taken as evidence of implied consent. Clearly this is dependent on adequate information having been provided at the start of the questionnaire or in the covering letter. However, if the study involves patients, invasive procedures, or collection of data from a third party then signed consent will always be necessary (Royal College of Physicians 1990).

The third set of ethical questions is concerned with the welfare of research participants. What will participating in the research involve? How much will participants be inconvenienced? What are the risks? It was pointed out above that many participants are likely to take on trust that the research is important and well conducted. This means that there will be no more inconvenience to participants than is absolutely essential, and that any discomfort and risks will be kept to a minimum. Furthermore, if any participant does suffer in any way, then arrangements must exist for minimizing the harm and for making recompense. It also means that if there is any potential for harm to participants, however slight, then the inconvenience and risks have been weighed against the potential benefits of the research by an independent research ethics committee. The role and functions of such committees are discussed further

Box 4.1 Information sheet for participants in Dr Smith's study

STUDY OF ADVICE FOR PEOPLE WITH ASTHMA

What is the purpose of this study?

We have developed an audiotape and a booklet of advice for people with asthma. The purpose of this study is to find out how helpful they are.

What will be involved if I agree to take part in the study?

The research assistant will visit you at home, explain the study to you and teach you how to use a peak flow meter. (A peak flow meter is a device for measuring how fast you can blow out). Later you will be sent a questionnaire in the post. You will be asked to complete this and for 10 days to make a record of your peak flow meter recordings, symptoms and medication. You may then be sent a copy of the tape and booklet. Twelve weeks later you will again be asked to complete a questionnaire and to keep a record of your peak flow recordings, symptoms and medication for a further 10 days.

What other information will be collected in the study?

None.

Will there be any effects on my treatment?

No, your participation in this study will not affect the care that you receive from your doctor in any way.

Box 4.1 (cont.)

Can I withdraw from the study at any time?

Yes, you are free to refuse to join this study and may withdraw at any time or choose not to answer certain questions. You will receive the same care from your doctor whether you join the study or not.

Will the information obtained in the study be confidential?

All the information will be treated in confidence, and care will be taken so that individuals cannot be identified from details in reports of the results of the study.

Will anyone else be told about my participation in the study?

Your doctor knows that you have been approached and with your permission will be informed if you agree to participate. No one else will be told about your participation in the study.

below. However, the fact that an ethics committee has given approval for a research project to proceed does not in any way reduce the onus on the researcher always to act with the welfare of participants uppermost in mind.

A particular concern arises in the case of research which seeks to compare a new treatment or intervention with an existing one. There is now wide consensus that the intervention chosen for comparison should represent current best practice. Anything less would mean that patients receiving the comparison treatment would be disadvantaged as a result of participating in the research. Furthermore, if the new treatment is shown to be more beneficial than the comparison treatment, this conclusion will be of no significance for the future management of patients if the latter treatment does not represent best practice at the time of the research. These considerations mean that placebo-controlled studies on patients are only justified if clear reasons exist for believing that no current treatment is effective. This is obvious in the case of studies of drug treatment, but is not always so clear if the intervention is of another form, such as counselling or physiotherapy.

An issue that may arise in survey research is that of the participant who describes symptoms suggestive of serious disease, but who has not sought medical attention. Alternatively, a participant may disclose significant emotional distress, or a history of abuse or other traumatic experience. All these situations raise the question of what the researcher should do next. Plans for responding appropriately and responsibly should be worked out in advance and incorporated in the research proposal.

Research involving the collection of data from or about patients, or involving invasive procedures on volunteers, will normally require approval from a properly constituted research ethics committee with responsibility for the geographical area where the study will be conducted. The requirements of such committees do vary, but all will require submissions for approval to include the following:

- full copy of research proposal;
- copy of information sheet(s) for potential participants;
- copy of consent form(s);
- copies of any data collection instruments, such as self-administered questionnaires, or interview guides.

More detailed guidance about requirements will be available from the clerk or secretary to the committee. It is often also worth seeking advice from colleagues with previous experience of obtaining approval from the local committee. This is because ethics committees do vary somewhat in matters such as the extent to which they expect various issues to be explained and discussed in the proposal.

The process of obtaining approval from an ethics committee is seen by some researchers as a chore. This is shortsighted. The members of research ethics committees are usually experienced researchers who can make useful comments on the proposals that they consider. In addition, paying attention to the questions discussed above will enhance the scientific quality of a study in addition to its ethical status.

External stakeholders

External stakeholders are those people who are not members of the project team but who fall into one of two categories:

- their actions may significantly affect the progress of your project;
- the outcomes of your project may have implications for their future.

Some stakeholders may fall into both categories. It is worth taking time to reflect on who are your external stakeholders, and in what ways they may affect or be affected by your work. A useful structure for such reflection is given by Murphy *et al.* (1992). Having listed your stakeholders, try to answer the following questions for each of them:

- what is this individual/group's current involvement in the proposed research setting?
- what might the benefits of the research be to this individual/group?
- what might the costs of this research project be to this individual/group? Such costs may include time, disruption, financial loss and exposure;
- what power does this individual/group have to affect the success of the research adversely?

One powerful and interested stakeholder is likely to be your funding agency. By controlling access to your budget it can exert considerable influence on the progress of your work. In addition, it may have an interest in your findings and their policy implications. Other stakeholders may be colleagues who work in the same organization as you but who have no particular interest in your project. They may control access to facilities you require, or put demands on your time that conflict with the project timetable. If you are undertaking evaluation research then the people currently providing the service or function that is under evaluation are likely to be both powerful and interested stakeholders. Not only will they typically exert control over the ease with which you can collect data, but they will have a considerable vested interest in the findings and outputs of your project.

Having identified your significant external stakeholders you should consider whether you need to involve them in the planning process. Particularly in the case of commissioned research (when the original research question was posed by the funding agency) it is worth arranging a meeting with representatives of the commissioning agency, with the following objectives:

- to agree the objectives of the proposed research, and to ensure that there is mutual understanding of what the stated objectives actually mean;
- to agree what form the output or outputs will take and the quality criteria by which they will be judged.

Unless you achieve consensus on these points it is quite probable that the study you undertake will not answer the questions that the commissioning agency requires to be answered, and that they will be disappointed with the report and other outputs of your project. Conversely, if your key stakeholders have been involved in defining the research question and in specifying the outcomes of the project from an early stage then they are likely to feel a sense of ownership of the study, its findings and its outputs. It is important to document everything that you have agreed with your funding agency and any other stakeholders.

External stakeholders, especially those directly involved in the research setting, may be aware of significant practical constraints which may affect your proposed study. They may also have access to resources which could help. Such information is well worth time and effort invested at an early stage in meeting with such people or groups, explaining the research, and seeking their support. Where access to information or participants must be negotiated with gatekeepers, as discussed in Chapter 2, they too should be contacted at as early a stage as possible, and their support obtained. It is always easier to obtain support and assistance from people who know that they have had the opportunity to influence the design of a project at an early stage – preferably before the final formulation of the research objectives.

When first making contact with gatekeepers, potential research participants and other external stakeholders, you will need to present your credentials as a researcher. People will want confirmation that their time will not be wasted, and that they can trust you to act honestly and professionally. Information about the organization in which you work and your role within it is important, as are headed notepaper, word-processed letters and punctual time-keeping. It may also be helpful to seek a local champion, someone who is known to your stakeholders and respected by them, and who is prepared to introduce you to them. Such introductions may be by telephone, by letter or in person.

It is sometimes helpful to set up a formal steering group of key external stakeholders. The membership of the steering group should include yourself, your collaborators and research staff, representatives of gatekeepers and research participants, and other powerful or interested stakeholders. Representatives of your funding agency may also expect to be included, especially in the case of commissioned research. A steering group should meet at least three times; initially to define the research question and objectives, subsequently to approve the study protocol and agree on quality criteria for the outputs, and towards the end of the project in order to comment on the draft report before it is finally submitted. The group may also meet at other times if this seems useful. Meetings of the steering group should be carefully minuted.

If you have a large number of external stakeholders it may be impracticable for them all to be represented on a steering group. An alternative management structure for the project is then to establish a relatively small steering group representing those stakeholders that are particularly powerful and interested in your study, and a larger reference group of other interested parties. The reference group may never meet, or may only meet once or twice during the project, but should be kept informed and consulted on key issues.

Obtaining funding

Unless your study is expected to consume very few resources, it is likely that you will need to obtain specific funding to meet the direct costs of the project. Opportunities for funding vary substantially from country to country, and from time to time, so that it is only possible to give fairly general advice here, using the situation in one particular country at one particular time (Britain in 1995) as an example. Unless you are already experienced in obtaining funding for research you should seek further advice from local colleagues.

In Britain the principle sources of research funds fall into four groups:

- foundations and charities;
- government departments, other governmental organizations and the European Community;
- research councils;
- commercial organizations.

Foundations and charities are invariably established with explicit objectives in mind, and if they fund research will do so in the light of these. Several directories exist of foundations, charities and similar not-for-profit organizations which offer research funding. These directories give information about the areas in which research will be funded, the funds that are available and whether submissions will be considered at any time or only at specific intervals.

Government departments, other governmental organizations such as the National Health Service Executive, and the European Community fund a considerable volume of health research. Often the questions they wish to address are quite specific and are dictated by issues of national or Community policy. In consequence, they typically fund research through a contracting process rather than through the provision of outright grants. The contracting process makes it much more likely that the researcher will be held to account for any variation from the protocol.

Research councils similarly specify priority areas for investigation that are linked to issues of national policy, but may also consider applications for funds to address other topics.

Commercial organizations exist to provide a financial return on their shareholders' investments. If they fund research it is usually to support the development or marketing of one of their products. In addition, some companies will consider funding research that is relevant to their products although not directly concerned with them, perhaps in order to promote their good name.

When considering an application, funding agencies will typically consider four questions:

- is this an important research question to answer?
- should we support a study that seeks to answer this question?
- will this particular study answer the question?
- do these investigators have the skills, resources and support from others to bring this study to a successful conclusion?

It will be clear from the above outline of sources of funds that each funding agency has its own agenda which is often quite specific. It is a waste of time seeking support for a study which clearly falls outside an agency's area of interest. Once you have selected an appropriate agency, you should set out to provide it with a clear answer to these four questions. Your proposal should explain:

• where current knowledge is deficient;
• why it is important to fill this gap;
• how your study will fill this gap;
• what the resulting benefits will be.

In your proposal you should justify the size of your sample, your staff requirements, and any expensive items in the budget. Other aspects of the protocol may also require justification and it is always worth seeking the advice of an experienced colleague on a proposal before submitting it for funding. If you are concerned that you may not be perceived as having sufficient skills and experience to undertake your proposed study, then options include:

• asking a researcher with an established track record in the field to join you as a co-investigator, or to act as a named adviser to the study;
• undertaking a pilot study to test your proposed methods, and including a description of this in your proposal.

There are a number of recurring reasons why research proposals are not successful in obtaining funding. Some of the commonest are listed below:

• the study falls outside the agency's area of interest;
• the agency's guidelines for applicants have not been followed;
• the research question (or research hypothesis) and study objectives are not clearly stated;
• the proposed research is not original, and a similar study has already been published, or is known to be underway elsewhere;

- the proposed sample size is not adequately justified, or the justification is inappropriate;
- other aspects of the proposed methodology are not seen as appropriate;
- important details of the proposed methodology are not described, or the description is ambiguous.

Before you finally submit your proposal, it may be useful to consider it in the light of each of the seven points listed above.

Recruitment and selection of project staff

The issue of assessing your staff requirements was discussed in the last chapter. The pros and cons were considered of recruiting staff directly, paying an agency to provide staff, or obtaining help from existing staff within your organization. This section will describe in more detail the process of recruiting staff directly. Recruitment and selection is a complex area and in many countries is subject to equal opportunity laws and other legislation. Your organization should have recruitment and selection policies and procedures that have been constructed in the light of the legal requirements. You must therefore seek local advice from within your organization. What follows is a guide to the basic components of the process.

The recruitment and selection process has four stages:

- preparation of a job specification (duty statement);
- preparation of a person specification;
- recruitment of applicants for the post;
- selection from amongst the applicants.

An example of a job specification is given in Box 4.2, which gives details of the job under a range of headings. Those listed in the box are typical, although an individual organization may have its own pro forma.

Box 4.2 Detailed job specification for Dr Smith's research assistant

Job title
Research assistant

Purpose
To support the project leader, Dr Smith, in undertaking a study of the benefits of education about their disease for young adults with asthma.

Salary scale
University grade 1B pro rata

Duration of post
Eighteen months

Hours per week
50 per cent part time, hours to be negotiated

Leave entitlement
Four weeks per year annual leave, plus public holidays

Location
As specified

Responsible to
Dr Smith, project leader

Duties
To undertake such duties as the project leader directs, including:

• liaising with local general practitioners;
• contacting, visiting at home and recruiting study participants;
• preparing and distributing questionnaires and other material;
• coding and entering data on computer;
• assisting with data analysis;
• assisting with preparation of final report, including word processing and simple desk-top publishing.

> **Box 4.3 Person specification for Dr Smith's research assistant**
>
> *Essential qualities*
>
> - good written and spoken English;
> - keyboard skills, including basic word processing;
> - good interpersonal skills, including telephone skills;
> - evidence of dependability and thoroughness;
> - possession of a current driving licence and access to a car which can be used for the project.
>
> *Desirable qualities*
>
> - advanced word processing skills;
> - desk-top publishing skills;
> - previous experience of health service research;
> - experience of simple data analysis.

One reason for writing a detailed job specification is that it enables you to identify the skills and other attributes that will be required of the person who is appointed. These make up the person specification; Box 4.3 gives an example. Notice that the qualities required are divided into two groups, essential and desirable, and are described in a way that renders each of them potentially measurable.

Recruitment refers to the process of obtaining applications for your post. This is likely to involve advertising and your organization may well have a policy in relation to this. Your personnel department will certainly have experience of recruiting by advertisement and by other means and you should seek their advice about where and how to advertise. The detailed job specification will provide the basis for information to be included in the advertisement. Your personnel department may also be able to suggest other ways of recruiting applicants. It is often worth seeking applications from people who have been working on other research projects which are coming to an end. Another fruitful source of applicants is graduates from relevant degree courses. Copies of the job specification and person specification should be sent to people who express an interest in the post. When they apply formally, they can then provide information about themselves in the light of these specifications.

You will need to set a deadline after which applications for the post will not be considered. Once the deadline is past you can start the process of selecting the applicant to whom you will offer the post. Selection has two phases: short-listing and interviews. Short-listing is based on the information provided in writing by applicants. This information is compared with the essential qualities in the person specification, and a list is drawn up of those people who on the evidence provided, meet these criteria.

People whose names appear on the short list are normally invited for interview. They may also be required to undertake other selection tests, such as a test of keyboard skills, or to bring examples of previous work. In addition, reports may be sought from referees. The offer of appointment is made in the light of the evidence available from these various sources. The essential feature of the selection process is that each application is considered in the light of the qualities listed in the person specification, and the post is finally offered to the person who best meets these criteria. The whole process of recruitment and selection should be informed by a clear, explicit and comprehensive person specification, and you should be prepared to justify your decisions in the light of this.

It is worth remembering that during the selection process, applicants are also deciding whether or not they would wish to take up an offer and to work with you and other members of your organization. They should therefore be given an opportunity to ask questions, to have a look around, and perhaps to obtain information about the post in other ways.

5

Undertaking the project

Even the simplest project requires management of research activity, time, money and other non-human resources. Most projects also involve management of relationships with members of the project team and with external stakeholders. This chapter will address the processes of managing activity, time and money, and will describe a decision-making model for addressing problems in these areas. Management of relationships within the project team and with other stakeholders will then be discussed. The main questions that you should keep in mind during this phase of the project are summarized in Box 5.1.

Managing activity

Chapter 3 described the process of breaking a research project down into activity steps, each of which must be completed if the study objectives are to be achieved. Once the project is underway, then each step requires planning in more detail. The degree of planning will depend on the precise nature of the step itself but will address two questions:

Box 5.1 Research project manager's *aide-mémoire*

Activity
- what still needs to be done?
- by whom?
- how?

Time
- how much is there left?
- will this be enough?

Outcomes
- are the study objectives being achieved?
- will the outputs, if any, be produced?
- will the quality criteria be met?

Relationships
- what do I need to do concerning other members of the project team?
- what should I do concerning external stakeholders?

Money
- how much is there left?
- what still needs to be paid for?

- what are the objectives of this activity step?
- how will these objectives be achieved?

The answer to the first question will be determined by the objectives of the study as a whole, and by any quality criteria that have been defined for the outputs of the project. The attributes of a well-formed activity step objective are as follows:

- a clear, unambiguous statement is given of what will be achieved;
- criteria are included for determining whether the objective has been achieved;
- a deadline is included for when the objective will be achieved;
- the objective is seen as achievable by those on whose actions it depends;
- the objective is acceptable to those on whose actions it depends.

The answer to the second question will be constrained by the time and resources that are allocated to the activity step in question, and by other local circumstances. In answering the two questions you should seek to involve all those whose actions will contribute to the activity step. In this way you will bring the perspectives and experience of others to bear on the planning process, and will also foster a sense of ownership and commitment amongst those concerned (see Box 5.2).

Once the activity step is underway then it is important to monitor progress in order to ensure that the plan is being adhered to and that the objectives will be met. The amount of time and attention to detail required in monitoring will depend on the nature of the activity step, and the number and competences of the people that are involved. Processes of managing relationships between team members are discussed in the final section of this chapter.

Managing time

If your project is to be completed on time, then ideally it should run to timetable throughout. If activity lags behind schedule then you need to be aware of this at the earliest possible stage in order to take some kind of corrective action. There are two basic tools for monitoring actual activity against the planned schedule. The first of these is the Gantt

Box 5.2

One of the first steps in Dr Smith's project involves the production of an educational audiotape. She arranges a meeting between:

- her research assistant;
- a colleague with a particular interest in health education, who has offered to help write the script for the tape;
- the actor who is going to read the script;
- a friend who has expertise in the areas of production, sound engineering and editing.

They agree that the objective of the activity step is 'to produce, within budget and on time, an audiotape about their disease that is suitable for sending to young adults with asthma'.

At the end of their meeting, an action plan is agreed. Each of the five has a firm commitment to this plan and a clear idea of what he or she has to do in order to implement it.

chart which was introduced in Chapter 3. As each activity step listed on the chart is completed, so a coloured line is drawn above the solid line that was inserted during the planning phase. The result is a visual display of what was planned, what has been achieved, and any areas of delay that require attention.

An alternative monitoring tool is a milestone chart. Box 5.3 shows an example. The left-hand column is a list, in time order, of key events (milestones) that must be achieved if the project is to be a success. The middle column shows the scheduled completion date for each milestone and the right-hand column shows the actual date of completion. The result is a concise record of the progress of the project.

Although both a Gantt chart and a milestone chart provide a record of progress to date, their most important

Box 5.3 Example of a milestone chart for Dr Smith's project

Milestone	Completion date (weeks after start of project)	
	Scheduled	Actual
Audiotape produced	8	
Written material produced	8	
Research ethics committee approval obtained	8	
General practitioners recruited	8	
Interview schedule developed and piloted	8	
Sample drawn of young adults with asthma	10	
Participants recruited and consent obtained	26	
Pre-intervention data collected	30	
Participants randomized and educational package distributed	32	
Pre-intervention data coded and entered	34	
Post-intervention data collected	48	
Post-intervention data coded and entered	52	
Data analysis complete	64	
Participants and GPs thanked for their help	66	
Final report prepared and delivered	72	

function is to provide a structure for looking ahead. For example, as a milestone completion date draws near so this should be taken as a reminder to check that the relevant activity step will be completed on time. There is little point in waiting until the scheduled completion date has been reached before responding to a delay. A model for decision-making when the project starts to run behind schedule is described below.

Managing the budget

Research projects not uncommonly run into problems because actual expenditure exceeds what was planned. The elements of your budget over which you are likely to have most control during the study are those referred to in Chapter 3 as capital costs and other direct costs. Once you have recruited and appointed any research staff, then the budget for staff costs will be committed.

Your original budget statement recorded how much you allocated to each heading, or budget line. As the project progresses you will need a method of monitoring what has been spent, and therefore what remains. This is done using budget control charts. There are two kinds of these.

The first type of budget control chart is similar in some ways to a milestone chart. An example is shown in Box 5.4. The activity steps of the project are listed in the left-hand column. The next column shows the direct cost budgeted for each step. The column after that shows the actual direct cost of each step. The difference between the two is known as the variance and is recorded in the next column. The budgeted remaining balance is recorded next, then the actual balance, and finally the total variance is recorded in the final column. This last figure, the total variance, is calculated as the total of the individual activity step variances in column 4. It should also be equal to the difference between the budgeted remaining balance and the actual balance remaining, and this equality can be used as a check on the calculations. The final column is important because it shows the amount by which the total balance exceeds or falls short of budget.

Budget control charts such as that illustrated in Box 5.4 are widely used. However they can be difficult to interpret when more than one cost generating activity step is being undertaken at the same time. Another difficulty in their

Box 5.4 One form of budget control chart, showing the other direct costs of Dr Smith's project

Activity step	Direct cost			Remaining balance		
	Budgeted	Actual	Variance	Budgeted	Actual	Variance
Starting balance				4520	4520	0
1	1350			3170		
2	500			2670		
3	0			2670		
4	140			2530		
5	0			2530		
6	150			2380		
7	1230			1150		
8	370			780		
9	10			770		
10	100			670		
11	0			670		
12	330			340		
13	0			340		
14	0			340		
15	250			90		
16	90			0		

use is that the remaining balance and total variance columns reflect the total budget and give no information about what has happened in relation to different budget headings. Box 5.5 gives an example where the balance is greater than expected so that the total variance is positive. However, this hides the fact that the recording studio cost less than expected, while the printing and copying budget has been overspent. It would be important to know this for two reasons:

- if actual printing and copying costs continue to exceed the printing and copying budget then in time the total cost of the project may exceed the total budget;

> **Box 5.5 Illustration of how the total variance can be positive despite certain of the actual costs exceeding budget**
>
> In this example from Dr Smith's project, the cost of the recording studio was £600 (budgeted £900 – see Box 3.6) while printing and copying costs for activity step 1 totalled £100 (budgeted £50). The other costs for step 1 were as per budget, giving a total actual cost for the step of £1100 (budgeted £1350). The printing and copying costs for step 2 were £450 (budgeted £400) while the other costs were as budgeted, giving a total cost of £550 (budgeted £500). The function of a budget control sheet is to highlight developing problems so that action can be taken, whereas the positive total variance at the end of step 2 conceals the excessive costs of printing and copying.
>
> | Activity step | Direct cost | | | Remaining balance | | |
> |---|---|---|---|---|---|---|
> | | Budgeted | Actual | Variance | Budgeted | Actual | Variance |
> | Starting balance | | | | 4520 | 4520 | 0 |
> | 1 | 1350 | 1100 | 250 | 3170 | 3420 | 250 |
> | 2 | 500 | 550 | (50) | 2670 | 2870 | 200 |
> | 3 | 0 | | | 2670 | | |
> | 4 | 140 | | | 2530 | | |

- the funding agency may not permit transfer of costs, or virement, from one budget heading to another.

An alternative form of budget control chart is shown in Box 5.6. A separate chart of this form is made up for each budget heading. The third column shows the items whose costs have been allocated to that budget line and the second column shows the activity steps for which the items were required. The first column shows the dates on which the costs of the items were incurred. The fourth column gives the actual cost of each item and the fifth column

Box 5.6 Alternative form of budget control chart

The printing and stationery costs from the first two steps of Dr Smith's study are used here in illustration. Notice how the financial resources that remain available to the project can be read off the sheet at any time.

A separate chart of this form is made up for each budget heading.

Date	Activity step	Item	Cost	Balance
Starting budget			—	850.00
5/6/95	1	Inserts for audiotapes	100.00	750.00
12/7/95	2	Accompanying written material	340.00	410.00
19/7/95	2	Printing of folders to hold tapes etc.	110.00	300.00

gives the remaining balance in that part of the total budget. It is important to enter items and their costs as the latter are incurred rather than when payment is made. The financial resources that remain available for the project can be read off the control sheet directly and without further calculation. Although not shown in the example, it is also possible to include further columns showing the budgeted cost of each item, the cost variance (budgeted cost minus actual cost) for each item, the budgeted remaining balance and the variance from this of the actual remaining budget. In practice, these columns are rarely included, and many researchers find budget control charts of the form illustrated in Box 5.6 adequate for their needs.

Both the budget control systems described above are adequate for monitoring what you have spent, and thus what remains, out of your total budget. If you work in a university or other institution which can accept income and make payments on your behalf then this is all that you need. If you are personally responsible for the latter activities then you will need to keep a more complete set of books, either by hand or on computer. At a minimum you should start a journal of income and expenditure. This comprises two sections. The section referring to income has four columns:

- date;
- source of income (debtor);
- amount received;
- total income since start of project (or since start of current accounting period).

The section recording expenditure also has four columns:

- date;
- creditor;
- amount owed/paid;
- total expenses since start of project (or since start of current accounting period).

A more complete set of books would have additional sections (ledgers) for each debtor and creditor. This is known as a 'double entry' bookkeeping system, and is the system supported by virtually all accounting software.

The arithmetical relationship between your budget control sheets and the books is that, after allowing for any income not yet received and any payments not yet made (see the next paragraph concerning these) the remaining balance on the control sheets should equal that recorded in the books. However, the function of the former is to make clear how much money remains to meet the remaining costs of the project. The latter record cash flows in the past.

It may be that your funding agency will provide all the cash up front and will expect you to refund any remaining balance at the end of the project. However, they may provide some cash initially and further amounts on receipt of evidence of relevant expenditure, or they may pay all cash in arrears. In any case, it is wise to record income in your books only on receipt. Expenses, however, should be

Box 5.7 Example of a problem definition

Dr Smith notices that her printing and copying costs have exceeded what were expected during activity steps 1 and 2. Even if the remaining printing and copying costs do not exceed those predicted for steps 3–16, that part of her budget will still be overspent by £100. At the moment she has saved £300 on the cost of the recording studio, so that the total variance remains positive.

On further analysis, the reason why the actual costs of printing and copying are higher than expected is that Dr Smith has based her estimates on a printer's price list that is two years out of date.

recorded as soon as they are incurred. If they have not yet been paid, they should be encumbranced. That is, the amount should be entered with an X next to it, or other indication that the bill is still to be paid. When it is, the X is removed. Encumbrancing ensures that you are aware of all costs incurred to date, not just those for which money has changed hands.

Decision-making when problems arise

Problems arise during the most carefully planned research project. The objectives of an activity step are not met, the project begins to run over schedule, or actual costs exceed those that were predicted. One of the functions of the monitoring processes described above is to assist you in detecting when things are not going according to plan, at the earliest possible stage and when the problem is likely to be at its most soluble.

Once you have detected a problem, it is worth spending time investigating, thinking and talking about it so that you have a clear idea of all the relevant issues: the problem definition (see Box 5.7).

Although the process of defining the problem may suggest an obvious solution, it is often useful to brainstorm three or four different options. A helpful tool for deciding between the options is a decision matrix, shown in Box 5.8. This has four columns. In the first column are listed the possible options for responding to the problem. In the next are the implications of each option for the research objectives and outputs of the project. The next column lists the implications for the timetable, and the final column the implications for the budget. When identifying the implications of each option in relation to each of these three headings, it is often helpful to think first of the possible advantages of choosing that option, then the disadvantages. Clearly, several minds are better than one, and if possible you should involve others in the process of generating options and identifying their implications. Once an option has been selected, it is useful to define an objective and agree upon an action plan in the same way as was described above in relation to planning activity steps.

Managing relationships

Many health research projects involve more than one research worker, so that a project team of two or more is responsible for the work. The importance of working with other members of the project team in planning activity, and in addressing problems, has already been stressed. Whenever more than one person is involved in undertaking a research project then it is useful to have regular team meetings. These meetings will typically have the following items on the agenda:

- review of progress in relation to plan;
- review of any problems encountered and how they were handled;
- setting of objectives for next activity step(s);
- action planning for next activity step(s).

Box 5.8 Decision matrix for problem solving

Dr Smith and her research assistant identify three possible options for responding to the problem defined in Box 5.7 and then construct the following decision matrix:

Option	Implications for research objectives and outputs	Implications for timetable	Implications for budget
Take no action	None	None	Will remain within total budget if all other costs tightly controlled
Use a cheaper printer	Quality of outputs may be reduced	None	Will remain within total budget if all other costs accurately estimated
Save money on postage by using second class	Response rates to pre- and post-intervention surveys may be reduced	Slight delays in collecting data	Will remain within total budget if all other costs accurately estimated

In the light of the above, Dr Smith and her colleague decide to take no further action at present, but to be extra vigilant in monitoring printing, copying and other costs for the remainder of the study.

Your role in these meetings is likely to include the following:

- listener
  - what has been achieved?
  - what problems have there been?
  - what ideas have others brought to the meeting?
  - how do people feel about progress to date?

- facilitator
  - what questions do others have?
  - what suggestions do they have?

- contributor
  - what ideas and suggestions do you have?

- manager
  - who is going to do what?
  - when are they going to do it by?
  - how are they going to do it?
  - what resources are they going to do it with?

- integrator
  - what are the implications of the day to day decisions and actions for the overall completion of the project, within budget and on time?

- leader
  - which actions require positive feedback and praise?
  - which actions require critical feedback and discussion of future changes?
  - in what ways can you maintain and enhance commitment and morale?

It is a good idea to have an explicit agenda for project team meetings, either circulated for agreement during the previous couple of days, or agreed at the beginning and written on a whiteboard. Somebody should be nominated to keep minutes, and these should be produced and circulated to all present within the following few days. A convenient form of minutes is as action notes, with a list of agreed tasks and identification of who is responsible for undertaking them.

Even if you are the sole researcher it is likely that the actions of other people will have an impact on your work, or that the outcomes of your project will affect others in some way. The importance of identifying, considering and possibly involving these external stakeholders was discussed in the last chapter. It was suggested that you might consider setting up a steering group. This would meet initially to define the research question and objectives, meet again to approve the study protocol and agree on quality criteria for the outputs, and finally meet towards the end of the project in order to comment on the draft report before it is submitted. Once again, an agenda and minutes are essential. In order to avoid future misunderstandings, the minutes in this case should record agreements reached as well as actions to be taken.

You may feel that a steering group is not needed for your project. Even if you do set one up, not all of your external stakeholders are likely to be represented. Nevertheless, your relationship with these stakeholders and their relationship with your project will still require thought and careful management. It is worth taking pains to ensure that others are adequately informed about the project. Depending on the organization in which you work, the nature of your research and your existing relationship with your external stakeholders, you may consider giving one or more presentations or research seminars. Alternatively, you could distribute a regular newsletter, or occasional updates. If at all possible, you should make a particular point of thanking gatekeepers and participants for their help, and offering some feedback about the study and its findings. This last point will be taken up in the next chapter.

6

Finishing the project

Once you have completed your data collection and analysis you will be able to start drawing conclusions and exploring the implications of these. The first section of this chapter will describe an approach to this process. If your conclusions are to be heard and acted upon by others then they must be disseminated. Other people must be informed of their existence and convinced of their value. The second section of the chapter will address the issue of disseminating your research findings. The third section will be concerned with marketing any other outputs of your project; Dr Smith's educational package will be used as an example. The final section will address the question of project evaluation; what lessons can you take from the project that you will be able to apply to your future research?

Drawing conclusions and making recommendations

You are less likely to miss obvious conclusions if you approach your findings systematically, and if you involve others in the process. A suggested scheme for drawing conclusions from your results is outlined below:

- following on from your analysis, identify and list your main findings;
- reflect on the major threats to the internal validity of your study. That is, taking each of your key findings in turn, consider possible reasons why it may not be valid;
- refresh your memory of the relevant literature and if necessary update your review of this;
- now consider each of your key findings in the light of other published research; in what ways have you advanced knowledge?
- write down your conclusions in the light of your own research findings and of the published work of others.

If your work is to inform the actions of others then you also need to discuss the implications of your conclusions, and perhaps make firm recommendations as a result. Implications and recommendations will typically fall into two categories:

- implications and recommendations for future practice and policy;
- implications and recommendations for future research.

Your recommendations will flow from your conclusions and a useful technique is to ponder each conclusion in turn, thinking first about its implications for future practice and policy, and then the implications for further research.

Obviously if you have not been the only person involved in the research then all members of the team should be involved in drawing conclusions, reflecting on the implications and formulating recommendations. In the case of evaluation research, and in other situations where people other than members of the research team have a close interest in the project, then it has already been suggested that key stakeholders should be closely involved in the setting of research objectives, clarification of quality criteria and approval of the study protocol. It may also be valuable to involve such stakeholders in the process of defining conclusions, implications and recommendations. One approach is to organize a workshop in which you present your findings and then invite participants to work with you in this process. Another possibility is to prepare and circulate a draft report for stakeholders' comments and suggestions. Involving external stakeholders does not merely draw on a range of different perspectives in addition to your own, but also ensures that the participants are aware of your findings and have a degree of ownership of the conclusions and recommendations.

It was suggested at the end of the last chapter that it is appropriate where possible to thank everyone who has helped in some way with a research project, and to offer feedback about the study and its findings. If you are able to do this, by writing to survey respondents for example, then it may also be helpful to invite their views about the implications of your research.

Disseminating your research findings

Most health research is intended for public dissemination. If your recommendations are to be translated into action then a useful first step is to identify your target audiences; those groups and individuals who are the decision makers in the relevant areas of practice, policy and research. They may be fellow researchers, practitioners or government ministers but the aim is to persuade them to listen to your findings and act upon your recommendations. Having identified your target audiences you can then consider how best to inform them of your conclusions and recommendations, and convince them of the value of your research. Options include verbal presentations, papers in journals, and published or unpublished reports (Hawkins and Sorgi 1985; Hall 1994). Whichever methods you choose, each audience will expect you to address the following areas:

- the relevance of the topic under investigation; why is it important to the listener or reader?

- previous literature on the topic; what is the gap in current knowledge that needs to be filled? Why is it important to do so?
- the aim of the present study; how will it fill the gap?
- details of the research method (in a longer report such as a dissertation or thesis, it is often appropriate to explain why one particular method was chosen in preference to another);
- a clear account of the findings, sufficient for the reader to draw his or her own conclusions and also to justify those conclusions that you have drawn;
- discussion of the internal and external validity of the study, focusing on the key findings and drawing attention to both strengths and limitations of the work;
- discussion of these findings in relation to other published work;
- key conclusions;
- implications for practice, policy and further research.

Most funding agencies will require a final report. The format of this and the level of detail that is needed both vary enormously between different bodies, although all will expect information about findings, conclusions and implications. In addition, all will require some form of financial report. The final financial report from Dr Smith's study is shown in Box 6.1. Notice that the headings listed in the first column correspond to those listed in the budget for the project, as presented in the final proposal (Box 3.7). This style of final financial report is appropriate unless the funding body has different requirements, or the financial arrangements have been particularly involved.

Marketing the products of your project

Many research projects do not lead only to verbal presentations, reports to stakeholders and published papers. They may have other outputs such as educational material, a video or an unpublished written report prepared for an audience beyond the immediate stakeholders. If these

Box 6.1 The final financial report for Dr Smith's study

Final budget statement

Heading	Cost		
	Allocated	Actual	Variance underspend (overspend)
Research assistant	12 064.00	12 028.40	35.60
Superannuation etc.	3 137.00	3 117.65	19.35
Computer, printer and software	2 000.00	1 899.20	100.80
Recording studio	900.00	600.00	300.00
Audiotapes	300.00	315.00	(15.00)
Peak flow meters	960.00	939.50	20.50
Stationery	350.00	373.67	(23.67)
Printing and copying	850.00	884.73	(34.73)
Postage	570.00	562.25	7.75
Telephone	150.00	167.54	(17.54)
Travel and subsistence	440.00	532.89	(92.89)
Overheads	6 080.00	6 080.00	00.00
Total	27 801.00	27 500.83	300.17

products are to be used and acted upon then they must be marketed. There are four sets of variables which will affect the consumption of any product within its potential market (Forsyth 1993). Together these are known as the marketing mix:

- attributes of the product;
- promotion;
- price;
- availability.

The first set of variables are the attributes of the product itself. These include its presentation as well as its content.

Good quality presentation is likely to encourage use of the product while a poor standard may raise questions in users' minds about the quality of other aspects of the work.

Decisions about how the product will be promoted are crucial in determining how widely it becomes known and how much it is used. Clearly the publication of a research paper in a well-respected journal will be invaluable in raising the profile of the study as a whole. Presentations at scientific meetings are also important in raising the awareness of others. When thinking about promotion of the products of your study, it is useful to consider each one in turn. Try to define which group or groups of people are likely to be interested in it. Then try to identify a single attribute of the product that you think will be of particular interest to this group. This is sometimes known as its 'unique selling point', 'unique sales proposition' or USP. Finally, identify two or more different ways of informing this group about the product and its USP, examine the advantages and disadvantages of each option, and make a choice in the light of these. Box 6.2 gives an example of the process.

The third component of the marketing mix is the price at which the product is sold. In the case of published material it is the publisher who will set this. In the case of material that you will be promoting and making available yourself, you will need to consider whether you intend to charge, and if so how much. Most goods exhibit price elasticity, with a negative association between consumption and price. However, this is not always the case as a higher price is sometimes interpreted as a sign of superior quality, leading to higher consumption. In addition, the price–consumption curve may be virtually flat at low prices; having decided to buy, a purchaser may not be influenced by small variations. If you do decide to charge, it seems wise to cover at least the marginal cost of providing the product to a purchaser. The marginal cost represents the total of the costs that you would not incur if you did not supply the product. Typically these include the costs of stationery, printing or copying, packaging and postage. If you decide to charge more than the marginal cost of

Box 6.2

Dr Smith concludes from her study that her educational intervention is associated with improvements in several measures of participants' health and also in a reduction in acute attacks of asthma. She thinks it likely that this would lead to a reduction in calls for urgent medical treatment. She is keen to promote the uptake and use of her educational package in the light of these findings. Dr Smith realizes that there is a potential market amongst general practitioners. They would be interested in an educational intervention which improves their patients' health and would be particularly attracted by its potential to reduce urgent requests for treatment. Dr Smith identifies three ways of promoting her package:

Option 1

Contact a number of medical journalists, and tell them about the study and package with the intention of encouraging them to write an article in the medical press.

Advantages:
• cheap
• national coverage

Disadvantage:
• journalists may write articles critical of the product

Option 2

Place an advertisement in a publication that is read widely by general practitioners.

Advantages:
• national coverage
• control over content of the advertisement

Box 6.2 (cont.)

Disadvantages:
- cost
- advertisement may not be widely read

Option 3

Mail a 'flyer' (a single sheet of paper giving details of the product) directly to local general practitioners.

Advantages:
- control over content
- product may be perceived as of particular value because locally produced and tested

Disadvantages:
- cost
- limited coverage of potential market

After identifying the three options and reflecting on the advantages and disadvantages of each, Dr Smith chooses the first two. She decides to contact a number of widely-read medical publications with the intention of persuading them to carry an article about her educational package. She then plans to place an advertisement for the product in those publications that run the story.

supplying the product, then a useful guide to pricing is the price that others charge for similar products aimed at similar markets. You should remember that under certain circumstances you will be required to charge and account for sales tax, such as Value Added Tax in Britain, on part or all of the purchase price.

The final component of the marketing mix is the availability of the product. Obviously the more difficult it is to obtain a product, the fewer people will avail themselves of the opportunity. Conversely, a high degree of availability will increase consumption. You should think about whether it would be better to make the product available through an outside agency, or to have all enquiries and requests come to your own organization. If the latter, will you deal with these yourself, or should somebody else be designated? If somebody else is to respond to enquiries, what instructions and other training do they need?

The four elements of the marketing mix provide a structure for deciding how best to promote each of your products to each of the target groups that you have identified.

Project review and summative evaluation

This should be the final step of any project. The aim is to review the processes of study definition, planning, implementation and dissemination with a view to learning how these could be done better next time. The review should be undertaken by yourself and members of your project team, if any, working together as a group. It is useful to write down what has been learned for future reference. The following questions are suggested as a guide:

Research process:

- Did we miss any key publications in our initial literature review?
- What have we learned about undertaking a literature review?
- Did any of the research objectives require revision during the study?
- What have we learned about formulating research objectives?
- Did any of the quality criteria require revision?
- What have we learned about specifying quality criteria?
- Was the study completed under or over time?

- What have we learned about project scheduling?
- Was the study completed under or over budget?
- What have we learned about budgeting?
- Did we have to vary from the original protocol at any point? Why? What have we learned?

External relationships:

- Are any of our key stakeholders unhappy?
- If no, what did we do to ensure that this would be the case?
- If yes, is there anything we can do to recover the situation?
- What should we do differently in future?

Internal relationships:

- Is any member of the project team unhappy?
- If no, what did we do to promote this?
- If yes, is there anything we can do to improve matters?
- What should we do differently in the future?

Overall evaluation:

- If we had the opportunity to undertake the study again, what would we do differently?
- What would we do the same?

Conclusion

Health research is important for two reasons. The proper role of health services is to provide effective care that is relevant to the needs of the community, is accessible to all members of that community, and is delivered as efficiently as possible in order to maximize the benefits obtained from available resources. Research has an important part to play in informing the planning, implementation and evaluation of health service developments in order to meet these goals. In addition, the very process of undertaking health research engages investigators and other stakeholders in reflection and critical debate about fundamental issues of health and health care. If the conclusions of your study are to make a well-founded contribution to service development, and if your project is to provide a focus for rigorous discussion, then the application of appropriate methodologies must be supported by careful management of activity, time, resources and human relationships. The object of this book has been to provide a systematic approach to such management.

References

Abramson, J.H. (1984) *Survey Methods in Community Medicine*, Edinburgh, Churchill Livingstone.

Armitage, P. and Berry, G. (1987) *Statistical Methods in Medical Research*, Oxford, Blackwell.

Bennett, R. (1994) *Managing Activities and Resources*, London, Kogan Page.

Berk, R.A. and Rossi, P.H. (1990) *Thinking About Programme Evaluation*, Newbury Park, CA, Sage.

Bryman, A. (1988) *Quantity and Quality in Social Research*, London, Routledge.

Burke, R. (1992) *Project Management. Planning and Control*, Chichester, Wiley.

Dillman, D.A. (1978) *Mail and Telephone Surveys. The Total Design Method*, Chichester, Wiley.

Florey, C. du V. (1993) Sample size for beginners, *British Medical Journal*, 306: 1181–4.

Forsyth, P. (1993) *Marketing for Non-Marketing Managers*, London, Pitman.

Gardner, M.J. and Altman, D.G. (1989) *Statistics with confidence. Confidence intervals and statistical guidelines*, London, British Medical Journal.

Geddes, M., Hastings, C. and Briner, W. (1990) *Project Leadership*, Aldershot, Gower.

Hall, G.M. (ed.) (1994) *How to Write a Paper*, London, British Medical Journal.

Hawkins, C. and Sorgi, M. (1985) *Research. How to Plan, Speak and Write About It*, Berlin, Springer-Verlag.

Haynes, M.E. (1989) *Project Management*, London, Kogan Page.

Hopkins, L. (1994) *Budgeting for Business*, London, Kogan Page.

Hult, M. and Lennung, S.-A. (1980) Towards a definition of action research: a note and bibliography, *Journal of Management Studies*, 17: 241–50.

Judd, C.M. and Kenny, D.A. (1981) *Estimating the Effects of Social Interventions*, Cambridge, Cambridge University Press.

Kuzel, A.J. (1992) Sampling in qualitative enquiry, in Crabtree, B.F. and Miller, W.L. (eds) *Doing Qualitative Research*, Newbury Park, CA, Sage.

Moore, C.M. (1987) *Group Techniques for Idea Building*, Newbury Park, CA, Sage.

Murphy, E., Spiegal, N. and Kinmonth, A. (1992) 'Will you help me with my research?' Gaining access to primary care settings and subjects, *British Journal of General Practice*, 42: 162–5.

Patton, M.Q. (1990) *Qualitative Evaluation and Research Methods*, Newbury Park, CA, Sage.

Reason, P. (ed.) (1988) *Human Inquiry in Action: Developments in New Paradigm Research*, London, Sage.

Royal College of Physicians (1990) *Research Involving Patients*, London, Royal College of Physicians.

Strauss, A. and Corbin, J. (1990) *Basics of Qualitative Research. Grounded Theory Procedures and Techniques*, Newbury Park, CA, Sage.

Wager, E., Tooley, P.J.H., Emanuel, M.B. and Wood, S.F. (1995) How to do it. Get patients' consent to enter clinical trials, *British Medical Journal*, 311: 734–7.

Whitaker, V. (1994) *Managing people*, London, HarperCollins.

Yates, F. (1981) *Sampling Methods for Censuses and Surveys*, London, Griffin.

Further reading

This bibliography could not possibly list all the high quality books about research and research methods that are relevant to health research. What it does is to identify a small number that give useful advice in relation to particular types of research and research contexts. Publications that are cited in the list of references are not listed again here.

Armstrong, D., Calnan, M. and Grace, J. (1990) *Research Methods for General Practitioners*, Oxford, Oxford University Press.
Bell, J. (1987) *Doing Your Research Project*, Milton Keynes, Open University Press.
Blaxter, L., Hughes, C. and Tight, M. (1996) *How to Research*, Buckingham, Open University Press.
Bryman, A. (1989) *Research Methods and Organization Studies*, London, Routledge.
Buckeldee, J. and McMahon, R. (1994) *The Research Experience in Nursing*, London, Chapman and Hall.
Colquhoun, D. and Kellehear, A. (eds) (1993) *Health Research in Practice. Political, Ethical and Methodological Issues*, London, Chapman and Hall.
Easterby-Smith, M., Thorpe, R. and Lowe, A. (1991) *Management Research. An Introduction*, London, Sage.

Hart, E. and Bond, M. (1995) *Action Research for Health and Social Care*, Buckingham, Open University Press.

Morrell, D. (ed.) (1988) *Epidemiology in General Practice*, Oxford, Oxford University Press.

Ong, B.N. (1993) *The Practice of Health Service Research*, London, Chapman and Hall.

Orna, E. and Stevens, G. (1995) *Managing Information for Research*, Buckingham, Open University Press.

Popay, J. and Williams, G. (eds) (1994) *Researching the Peoples' Health*, London, Routledge.

Sapsford, R. and Abbott, P. (1992) *Research Methods for Nurses and the Caring Professions*, Buckingham, Open University Press.

Shakespeare, P., Atkinson, D. and French, S. (eds) (1993) *Reflecting on Research Practice: Issues in Health and Social Welfare*, Buckingham, Open University Press.

Index

DOING YOUR RESEARCH PROJECT (2nd edition)
A GUIDE FOR FIRST-TIME RESEARCHERS IN EDUCATION AND
SOCIAL SCIENCE

Judith Bell

If you are a beginner researcher, the problems facing you are
much the same whether you are producing a small project,
an MA dissertation or a PhD thesis. You will need to select a
topic; identify the objectives of your study; plan and design a
suitable methodology; devise research instruments; negotiate
access to institutions, material and people; collect, analyse and
present information; and finally, produce a well-written report
or dissertation. Whatever the scale of the undertaking, you
will have to master techniques and devise a plan of action
which does not attempt more than the limitations of
expertise, time and access permit.

Doing Your Research Project serves as a source of reference and
guide to good practice for all beginner researchers, whether
undergraduate and postgraduate students or professionals such
as teachers or social workers undertaking investigations in
Education and the Social Sciences. It takes you from the stage
of choosing a topic through to the production of a well-
planned, methodologically sound and well-written final report
or dissertation on time. This second edition retains the basic
structure of the very successful first edition whilst
incorporating some important new material.

Contents
*Introduction – Part I: Preparing the ground – Planning the project –
Keeping records and making notes – Reviewing the literature –
Negotiating access and the problems of 'inside' research – Part II:
Selecting methods of data collection – The analysis of documentary
evidence – Designing and administering questionnaires – Planning
and conducting interviews – Diaries – Observation studies – Part
III: Interpreting the evidence and reporting the findings –
Interpretation and presentation of the evidence – Writing the report
– Postscript – Bibliography – Index.*

192pp   0 335 19094 4 (Paperback)

ACTION RESEARCH FOR HEALTH AND SOCIAL CARE
A GUIDE TO PRACTICE

Elizabeth Hart and Meg Bond

- What is action research and how can it best be understood?
- How can practitioners use action research to deal with problems and improve services?
- What are the different types of action research and which might be most appropriate for use in a particular setting?

This book has been designed for use as a core text on research methods courses at undergraduate and postgraduate level and on professional training courses. It is divided into three parts. Part one traces the history of action research and shows the links between its use in education, community development, management research and nursing. Building on this background the book explores different ways in which action research has been defined and proposes four different types, each appropriate to a different problem situation and context. In part two, five case studies of action research are described from the perspective of the researcher, including case studies of success and instructive failure. Part three is designed to enable the reader to find a route through the maze of methods and approaches in action research by the use of such things as self-assessment and mapping exercises, a guide to diary keeping and to evaluation. The final chapter suggests that by developing a 'project perspective' action research can be of practical benefit to health and social care professionals in promoting service improvements.

Contents

256pp   0 335 19262 9 (Paperback)   0 335 19263 7 (Hardback)